What Is Sin?

What Is Virtue?

ROBERT J. McCRACKEN

What Is Sin?
What Is Virtue?

HARPER & ROW, PUBLISHERS, *NEW YORK*

FIRST EDITION

LIBRARY OF CONGRESS CATALOG CARD NUMBER: 66-15043

C-Q

Contents

Preface   7

THE SEVEN DEADLY SINS

  1. Pride 11

  2. Envy 17

  3. Anger 22

  4. Sloth 28

  5. Avarice 34

  6. Gluttony 39

  7. Lust 45

THE SEVEN CARDINAL VIRTUES

  1. Wisdom 53

  2. Justice 58

  3. Temperance 64

  4. Courage 71

  5. Faith 77

  6. Hope 83

  7. Love 89

Notes appear at the end of each chapter

Preface

FROM ancient times, seven has been a significant, sacred, and mystic number: seven days in creation, seven days in the week, seven planets, seven ages in the life of man, seven works of mercy, seven gifts of the Holy Spirit.

By the fourth century Christians were speaking of seven cardinal virtues. Wisdom, justice, temperance, and courage they took over from the pre-Christian world, and on them they put their own distinctive stamp. The remaining three, faith, hope, and love, which are graces as well as virtues, they brought out of their own treasury. Down the centuries all seven have been inculcated as the highest standard of behavior alike for personal character and an ordered and durable society.

The seven deadly sins have also had a long history. At the outset there was not the same unanimity among Christians as to what they are. Stress was placed first on the carnal sins: lust and gluttony. Later, attention was concentrated more on pride, envy, and anger. Later still, the emphasis shifted to avarice and sloth. It is noteworthy that neither untruthfulness nor dishonesty appeared on any list but that gloominess did. As an exercise in self-anatomy the reader of this book might well set up his own scale of priority and vulnerability.

Somehow the cardinal virtues lack the human interest of the deadly sins. One of the mysteries of preaching is that congregations seem to relish hearing about their sins. As with newspapers, novels, and plays, virtue is seldom as good copy as vice. Why is it so difficult to write an outstandingly good novel about a superlatively good character? Dostoievsky in *The Idiot* sought to do precisely that—as he put it, "to portray a truly beautiful soul"—but *Crime and Punishment* has all along had a much more popular appeal.

The question of contemporary relevance arises. Why should the virtues and vices expatiated upon by the ancients be made the

7

subject of study in our day? A character in Margaret Irwin's historical novel *The Proud Servant,* its background the seventeenth century, remarks, "Would that the cardinal virtues had gone out with the cardinals!" Rose Macaulay encountered an attitude of the same sort when broadcasting a series of talks on the seven deadly sins. There were critics who questioned the validity of all seven. Their questions call for answers and this book attempts to provide them. It is written out of a conviction that no less than our fore-bears we need direction in the forming of moral judgments. We need to know ourselves better than we do, to recognize and deal with the facts about our inner lives, both the good and the evil. Without self-diagnosis there can be no mental honesty, and mental honesty is the first requisite of mental, moral, and spiritual health.

The Seven Deadly Sins

The martyrs to vice far exceed the martyrs to virtue, both in endurance and in number. So blinded are we to our passions, that we suffer more to insure perdition than salvation. Religion does not forbid the rational enjoyments of life as sternly as avarice forbids them. She does not require such sacrifices of ease as ambition; or such renunciation of quiet as pride. She does not murder sleep like dissipation; or health like intemperance; or scatter wealth like extravagance or gambling. She does not embitter life like discord; or shorten it like revenge. She does not impose more vigilance than suspicion; more anxiety than selfishness; or half as many mortifications as vanity!

—HANNAH MORE

1. Pride

THE problem I face in writing about pride is that those who need to think about it most, as often as not assume that they do not need to think about it at all. They see how it applies to others but are insensitive to its application in their own case. The peculiar feature of pride, its insidious feature, is that one seldom comes across anybody acknowledging: This is my sin, my chief sin, my worst sin.

I recall preaching a sermon about the obligation we all feel to justify ourselves to others and to ourselves. In the course of it I said the things about pride which the Bible says and which the Church teaches; if we make a listing of our sins, a salutory discipline and one without which there can be no genuine self-knowledge, this is the one that heads the list, breeds all the rest, and does more to estrange us from our neighbors or from God than any evil we can commit. No sooner was I out of the pulpit than I was asked whether there was not a legitimate and worthy pride—pride in appearance, work, family, church, country. It would not have helped much to suggest that the point of the sermon had been missed, for that would have invited the reply that it should have been made so clear that nobody could miss it. Indeed, when I countered by inquiring if one ought to be conceited about one's appearance, work, family, church, country, the rejoinder was: Why didn't you preach about conceit? The questioner was off the hook and the preacher on the spot. The passion for self-justification is powerful, in the pulpit no less than in the pew.

The word *pride* has varied and contrasted shades of meaning. It does duty both for inordinate, overweening self-esteem and for a proper and Christian self-respect. On the one hand it denotes boasting, complacency, arrogance, and on the other an open-eyed recognition of one's capacities, skills, and God-given worth. The Bible, however, puts repeated emphasis on pride as having its root in self-centeredness. In this aspect, it is not only the worst of the seven deadly sins; it is the parent sin, the one that leads to every other, the sin from which no one is free. Mastery may be won over envy, anger, avarice, sloth, gluttony, lust, but who can claim that he is rid utterly and forever of the self-centeredness which makes pride the chronic evil it is? "This," writes John Whale, "is where man's personality is rotten at the core." C. S. Lewis is equally emphatic: "Unchastity, anger, greed, drunkenness and all that are mere flea bites in comparison with pride." Pascal defines pride as "essentially unjust in that it makes self the center of everyting, and it is troublesome to others in that it seeks to make them subservient." Aquinas offers a similar definition: "Every sinful act proceeds from an inordinate desire for some temporal good. The fact that one desires a temporal good inordinately is due to the fact that he loves himself inordinately."

The third chapter of the Book of Genesis contains a diagnosis of pride as in its essence the parent sin. Dramatized in the story of the Garden of Eden is the timeless truth that man, made to go God's way, has a besetting tendency to take his own way. In this sense Adam is Everyman and his experience the universal experience. Adam wills himself out of his subordinate relation to God. There is a fundamental egoism in him which impels him to put himself and his interests first. He proposes to be independent of God, the master of his fate and captain of his soul. It is the essence of man's pride to assume that he is self-sufficient and that by his efforts and skills he can take care of himself, order his affairs, do for himself all that has to be done. The serpent in tempting Adam and Eve promised: "You will be as gods." Here is the primary temptation, to put ourselves where God should be—at the center of things, to ignore our creatureliness and finiteness as though we were self-made and self-adequate, and assert our independence and sovereignty. Looking over his past life, Newman confessed, "I loved to see and choose my path. . . . Pride ruled my will." The reason why, as we grow older, many of us sing Newman's hymn with deep feeling is because we have to make the same confession. We put ourselves first, not God. What place has He in an average day, in our work, in our life plans? Do we depend on Him, obey Him, make our will subservient to His? Our bias is in the direction of self-interest, our dominant preoccupation is the independent ordering and management of our affairs and concerns.

This is what is meant by original sin, not a physical defect inseparable from sex and transmitted by Adam and Eve to their posterity, but a tendency common to men everywhere to put themselves in the place of God by setting themselves at the center of their world. Theologians speak of it as "original" because it is the primary cause of all evil. It is tragically deep-seated, for history attests that it cannot be extirpated by any effort of the will or by any human agency whatsoever. Socially as well as individually, it is the source of all our troubles, of the dissension and strife that go to the making of the human predicament. Since we are all alike in wanting to constitute ourselves the center of things, we are deeply divided from one another, our interests competing and clashing. Humanity presents a spectacle of confusion precisely because individuals are concerned principally about their own private good. Classes and nations, like individuals, are endemically egotistical:— *Deutschland über Alles,* Britannia Rules the Waves, America First. As a matter of practical politics, what nation ever operates on the principle that God has no favorites, that it is no more important than any other nation, that power is to be equated not with privilege and prerogative but with duty and responsibility? How can we expect anything but chaos if we attempt to give the world as many centers as there are nations—and individuals? The only center of the world is God, and until we recognize His centrality there can be no alleviation of the human quandary.

The reason why all who, thinking seriously about pride as the original sin, speak of it in somber fashion is that it takes an endless variety of forms. It attaches itself to and poisons every pursuit and activity of mankind. Pride of rank—the delight taken in status, recognition, honors, in being at the head of the table, the top of the line, the cynosure of all eyes. Pride of intellect—the arrogance that thinks it knows more than it does, forgets the finiteness of the human mind, talks in terms of morons, smiles at the cultural crudity of contemporaries, and needs to be told what Madame Foch said to one of her sons who was boasting about a school prize: "Cleverness which has to be mentioned does not exist." Pride of power—the passion to achieve it, to wield more and more of it, to feel superior to others, to give orders with a strident voice and move men about like pawns on a chessboard. Pride of nation—shot through with pretension and deception, resulting in the deification of the national interest, in definitions of good and evil which have little relation to universal moral law, in the egotism of the will-to-power asserting itself as a disinterested activity, modern imperialism the white man's burden, modern communism a crusade for social justice.

Worst of all is spiritual pride, exemplified in Christ's parable by an accredited representative of religion, a man who even in prayer is self-centered (yet who is not?)—who basks in the sunshine of his own approval, recalls his pieties and charities, dwells on the general excellence of his record compared with that of his neighbors, his twentieth-century counterpart the individual who says that he never goes to church but is as good as those who do, the type described by Alice Meynell:

> For I am tolerant, generous, keep no rules,
> And the age honors me.
> Thank God I am not as these rigid fools,
> Even as this Pharisee.[1]

A Sunday-school teacher at the end of a lesson on the proud Pharisee and the penitent Publican counselled her class to thank God that they were not like the Pharisee! The story goes that a Carthusian monk, explaining to an inquirer the distinctive feature of his Order said: "When it comes to good works, we don't match the Benedictines; as to preaching, we are not in a class with the Dominicans; the Jesuits are away ahead of us in learning; but in the matter of humility, we're tops."

> And the devil did grin
> For his darling sin
> Is the pride that apes humility.

For this deadliest of sins there is no simple and speedy remedy. One of the Puritans lamented that ridding oneself of it was like peeling an onion; for every skin taken off there was another beneath. Katherine Mansfield wrote in her *Journal:* "I wonder why it should be so difficult to be humble. I do not think that I am a good writer; I realize my faults better than anyone else could realize them. I know exactly where I fail. And yet when I have finished a story and before I have begun another, I catch myself *preening* my feathers. It is disheartening. There seems to be some bad old pride in my heart; a root of it that puts out a thick shoot on the slightest provocation. . . . One must learn, one must practice to *forget* oneself. . . . Oh God! I am divided still. I am bad. I fail in my personal life. I lapse into impatience, temper, vanity, and so I fail as thy priest."[2]

In that exercise in self-examination, not morbid and neurotic but rigorous in its honesty and candor, we see the dimensions of the problem. To face the ugly facts about ourselves and unmask the pride that is ingrained in us requires sincerity and courage. But when the facts are faced and the disguises one by one stripped away, what then? How is pride to be got rid of? The most hopeful line is to see ourselves against some luminous background, to confront ourselves with a standard of excellence that puts our self-centeredness to shame. This is what happens when we submit ourselves to the white, scorching purity of Christ. "Who shall stand when he appeareth?" "When I saw him I fell at his feet as one dead." Charles Lamb's statement of the case goes to the core of the matter: "If Shakespeare were to come into this room we should rise to our feet; if Christ were to enter we should fall upon our knees."

By a strange quirk in human nature people are severest in their denunciations of the sins to which they are themselves most vulnerable and prone. Yet, while assailing pride as a deadly evil, there was no shadow of a suggestion of it in Christ, no pride of rank, power, nation, religion. There was a sublime self-consciousness but no self-centeredness. He has had critics in plenty, but there are no valid grounds on which He can be accused of egoism. His shining secret lay in His complete dependence on God and His unfailing obedience to the will of God. The Fourth Evangelist represents Him as saying, "I do nothing of myself, but as the Father has taught me, I speak. I do always those things that are pleasing to him." This was what awed and humbled all the New Testament writers: "Even Christ pleased not himself." It is what we habitually do, think first and foremost of our own interest and advantage—but not He, never He. Even more by His deeds than by His words He brought to the world a new virtue, the virtue of Christian humility. It is the wonder of the divine humility, revealed in a manger at Bethlehem, in the life of a working man at Nazareth, in a ministry marked from first to last by self-emptying and self-giving, and supremely on the Cross at Calvary, that has led people in every age to pour contempt on all their pride.

Simon Peter, for example. There was a driving egoism in him which got the better of his youthful idealism. It was he who so far forgot himself as to blurt out, "Lord, we have left all and followed you; what are we to get?" But one day in a fishing boat there flashed into his soul a revealing ray from the presence of Christ, and he saw himself for the self-engrossed person he was, and at once he was on his knees exclaiming, "Depart from me, for I am a sinful man, O Lord." As with Peter so with Paul. Talk about pride! It is

writ large in the cataloguing of his distinctions—"of the stock of
Israel, of the tribe of Benjamin, a Hebrew of the Hebrews; as
touching the law a Pharisee; concerning zeal, persecuting the
church; touching the righteousness which is in the law, blameless."
The encounter with Christ on the Damascus road, however, put an
end to all such self-congratulation. The old pride, based on self-
ignorance, shrivelled and in its place grew a new and ever deepen-
ing humility. At the beginning of his Christian life he felt that he
was "unworthy to be called an apostle." Years passed and he
described himself as "less than the least of all saints." In the prison
at Rome, his life almost at an end, he said that he was "the chief of
sinners."

There is only one sure way of ridding oneself of pride. It is to
keep close to Christ and take from Him day by day the gifts He
never fails to offer: cleansing, pardon, and power. The sum of the
whole matter is expressed in four lines from Browning's *Saul:*

> And thus, looking within and around me, I ever renew
> (With that stoop of the soul which in bending
>   upraises it too),
> The submission of man's nothing-perfect to God's
>   all-complete,
> As by each new obeisance in spirit, I climb to His feet.

NOTES

[1] From "The Newer Vainglory," quoted in *Masterpieces of Religious Verse,*
J. D. Morrison, ed. (New York: Harper & Row, 1948), p. 397. Used by permission
of Burns, Oates & Washbourne, Ltd. and the Executors of Alice Meynell.

[2] Katherine Mansfield, *Journal* (New York: Alfred A. Knopf, 1936), p. 198.

2. Envy

HARD, harsh things have been said about envy, as a glance at the uses of the word in Bartlett's *Quotations* will show. For example: "Envy's a coal come hissing hot from hell," and "Envy, the meanest of vices, creeps on the ground like a serpent." The language is dated and strikes us nowadays as exaggerated. Envy is a fault, but surely a minor, not a major fault. This, though the common assumption, does not stand up to the facts. The lurid language used to describe it in an earlier day is understandable if we consider envy's mean progeny: peevishness, pettiness, bitterness, spite, malice.

A case in point is the story of Saul and David, which in the light it sheds on human character is timeless. Saul was drawn to David, became fond of him, made him his adjutant, assigned him a place where he might always be near him. But as Saul's health broke and as David's accomplishments increased, the friendship was first strained and then ruptured. Saul could not bear to have the younger man around, gave him a command in the field, hoping that the accidents of war would take his rival out of the way. Something ruinous and deadly—the name for it is envy—was going on inside Saul, was burning him up. What was going on inside him did more to break his health than his advancing years. Doctors dealing with similar symptoms today have to be versed in psychopathology.

What is at the root of envy? Underneath its surface manifestations is the fact of inequality. In the sight of God we are all equal, but in native endowment we are not equal. One man has brains to burn, another has only average intelligence. One woman looks like a queen; another—does not. One person has not had a day's illness in years, is hale in heart and limb; another goes through life blind or deaf or cruelly deformed. "One star differs from another in glory"—in the firmament and on Broadway.

Compounding the problem is another fact: about many of these inequalities there appears to be little that anybody can do. A student toils like a galley slave and gets a *B* minus, while alongside him sits a fellow student who without straining himself gets straight

A's. This is what arouses envy. We want to know why we can't have what others have, and then we become disgruntled because others have what we don't. Envy has been defined as the sin of the Have-nots against the Haves. Doubtless one reason why some say it has been decried too much is because to fret and fume about the lack of brains or robust health or beauty of face and figure is only "doing what comes naturally." In a hack writer, dreaming despite his pedestrian qualities of literary genius, is it not inevitable?

Nor is it only those who complain of having been given a bad break—poor health, personality defects, no educational or social opportunities, no love affairs—who are envious. If anything, this is a sin even more pronounced in the well-endowed. One marvels constantly at the cheerfulness of the handicapped. But there are brilliant people—authors, artists, professors, clergymen—whose lives are full of tension because of the greater brilliance of associates. Envy in their case is often fierce, vindictive, overpowering; the mind twisted, a grudge rankling in the heart, personal relationships poisoned. An Old Testament sentence is apposite in this connection: "Behold, Benaiah was honorable among the thirty, but he attained not to the first three." Of all places to test a person's character, that is the place. To get as far up the ladder as that, but fail to reach the top. To be so close to the very front rank, and yet not quite make it. It is what some find galling. Benaiah is described as an honorable man. He would have had to be honorable and magnanimous or he would have resented and in all likelihood denigrated and criticized the first three. Had he been emotionally and temperamentally immature they would have plagued the life out of him. Highly gifted men and women not infrequently betray evidence of arrested development, of emotional childishness; they are psychological cripples. Though they may not be aware of it, and might be the last to admit it, they nurse dark feelings of insecurity and inferiority, which find an outlet in cruel disparagement and even callous behavior.

If envy seems to us natural, and to have been decried too much—to be a sin but not a deadly sin—we should be at pains to observe the ways in which it works. It is a born rationalizer. It refuses to give credit where credit is due. It will not face facts, more particularly facts injurious to self-esteem. It does not concede that the successful person has justly earned and deserved the promotion that has come to him. The success is explained, explained away, as being due to lucky breaks. Influence was exerted on his behalf. He was born into a well-to-do family, attended an Ivy League college, got into the right fraternity, married the boss's daughter. What envy can't have it belittles or derides. It is the great leveller; if it can't level things up, it levels them down. Montaigne sees the envious as saying, "Since we can't attain to greatness, let us avenge ourselves by railing at it." In the lines of Pope envy walks incarnate:

> Damn with faint praise, assent with civil leer,
> And without sneering teach the rest to sneer;
> Willing to wound, and yet afraid to strike,
> Just hint a fault, and hesitate dislike;
> Alike reserved to blame, or to commend,
> A tim'rous foe, and a suspicious friend.[1]

Or, changing its tack, envy questions motive. Somebody does a good deed, breath-taking in its selflessness and generosity—so selfless and generous that it shames and convicts us of illiberality and meanness. God have mercy on us, we can raise a question about the deed by suspecting the motive. A friend showers us with kindness upon kindness, and we say, "I wonder what he wants." A church member with half our means contributes half as much again as we do, and we tell ourselves he is trying to make an impression. An envious mind becomes a twisted mind. When the woman with the alabaster jar of very expensive ointment poured it over the feet of Jesus, one of the disciples complained: "This ointment might have been sold for much and given to the poor." It should not be lost on us that it was Judas who debunked that generous act.

The mention of Judas is a reminder that the one who nurses envy is the one who is hurt most by it. Others are affected, personal relations are strained and may be broken, but the severest injury wrought is to the envious soul, the injury self-inflicted, the torture self-imposed. Envy exacts a heavy toll. It makes its victim petulant, jealous, spiteful, mean—whatever his height in feet and inches, pitifully small. Picture the face of Judas when he muttered, "This ointment might have been sold for much and given to the poor." Saul was a magnificent specimen of a man, with brains as well as brawn, but envy dwarfed him and contributed to his self-destruction. Can anyone say he is completely free from it? Free from lust? Perhaps. Free from avarice? Perhaps. But free from envy? To know one's own heart is to realize that it takes strength of character to rejoice in the greater success of a rival, a friend, a relative, without a touch of envy.

Is there a remedy for this sin? There are several. One way of mastering envy is to learn to accept oneself and one's gifts, however modest, and make the best of them. When I began to preach I was full of misgiving. Toiling over my sermons I needed no one to tell me that they were amateurish efforts compared with the sermons of my heroes, A. J. Gossip in Aberdeen and Harry Emerson Fosdick in New York. In those days reading Emerson on an open-eyed, realistic self-acceptance was a tonic. "Nothing is at last sacred but the integrity of your own mind." "Let a man then know his own worth, and keep things under his feet. Let him not peep or steal, or skulk up and down with the air of . . . an interloper in the world which exists for him." "There is a time in every man's education when he arrives at the conviction that envy is ignorance; that imitation is suicide; that he must take himself for better or worse as his portion, that though the wide universe is full of good, no kernel of nourishing corn can come to him but through his toil bestowed on that plot of ground which is given him to till."[2] That is one way of mastering envy.

Another is to school and discipline oneself to think more of the work to be done than of the status of the worker. John the Baptist was at the height of his influence when Jesus appeared, but from that moment his influence began to wane. It was not only that the crowds left him for Jesus—the best and most promising of his disciples went as well. Another type of man would have become embittered; not John. There is no trace in him of envy, of admiration gone sour, of status-seeking. There was exultation in the cry, "He must increase, but I must decrease." For the Baptist the only thing of consequence was that the purpose of God should be served.

> What matter, I or they?
> Mine or another's day,
> So the right word be said,
> And life the sweeter made?[3]

That is a second way of rooting out envy.

It points to a third: reliance on sources of strength outside oneself. If John was without a trace of envy it was because his character was reinforced by God. What might have been impossible through human effort became possible through divine inspiration.

Because envy is a cardinal sin, not venial but ruinous and deadly, we need the help of God in dealing with it; we need His mercy and grace. A man on whom I urged self-acceptance told me he had a self he loathed and from which he wanted to get away. I reminded him that he could never get away from himself, that God could help him in the fashioning of a self from which he did not have to get away, a self he could live with. This is the assurance given us by the Gospel of the grace of God. Paul summarized it in a sentence, "In him who strengthens me I am able for anything."

Why not try it? Why not put it to the test? In our battle with sin, the sin of envy, any sin, we can get down on our knees and ask God to help us. Each morning before we go out to do business in the world, we can seek His aid, can make reliance on His presence and power a rule of life, as much a rule of life as eating, working, talking. The experience of men and women down the centuries attests that, if we do, He will bring us through the battle—weary it may be, but *content*, undishonored, conquerors, more than conquerors.

NOTES
[1] Alexander Pope, "Prologue to Satires," in the *Epistle to Dr. Arbuthnot.*
[2] Ralph Waldo Emerson, *Essay on Self-Reliance.*
[3] John Greenleaf Whittier, "My Triumph."

3. Anger

ANGER is one of the commonest of sins. The ancient moralists made the point that it is the first perversion of human nature to show itself, that a child before it can speak can work itself up into a passion of fury. Anger, too, is one of the most enduring of sins; when other vices are dead in a man this one lives on, dominant and domineering. Anger, moreover, is the cause of other sins. A woman told how every time she and her husband quarrelled, exchanging hot, bitter words, he went out and got drunk. Another bemoaned, "I kept Lent well for the first two weeks, but then I lost my temper very badly with my husband, and my religion went all to pieces."

There are two kinds of anger, the blazing kind and the brooding kind. Some of us are like gunpowder; the least little spark starts an explosion. If only we could see ourselves, our brow contracted, our eyes flashing, our features distorted! After flying into a towering rage many a man has to confess to himself, and may have the grace to confess to his victim, "I have made an ass of myself"—which is unfair to that animal! Some of us smoulder with temper, like the embers of a fire where there is no flame. Silent and sullen, we sulk over some wrong, real or imaginary, that has been done us. Whatever our individual propensity, most of us would rather deal with the person whose temper flares up and just as swiftly dies down than with the person who goes about nursing a grudge for whole days on end.

The humiliating thing is that so much of our anger is sparked by trifles. We are dressing in a hurry and our shoelace breaks. The traffic light goes green and the driver in the car ahead seems half-asleep at the wheel. A man goes into his office (this actually happened) and starts cursing because the wind from an open window has blown the papers off his desk and about the room. His secretary follows at his heels, and the tale of woe she carries home at the day's end loses nothing in the telling. She "gets mad" too, but not at papers lying all over the floor! George Eliot has a sentence, written either out of experience or observation, or both: "Very slight things make epochs in married life." Indeed they do. A woman was driven to write this diatribe about her husband:

> Some fretful tempers wince at every touch,
> You always do too little or too much;
> He shakes with cold; you stir the fire and strive
> To make a blaze; that's roasting him alive.
> Serve him with venison, and he chooses fish;
> With sole; that's just the sort he would not wish.
> Alas! his efforts double his distress,
> He likes yours little, and his own still less.
> Thus, always teasing others, always teased,
> His only pleasure is—to be displeased.[1]

I fear that I am handling this sin with too light a touch. And yet, I wonder? "A soft answer," the Bible says, "turns away wrath." So does a sense of humor. It is a saving grace. If I had my way I would make it a cardinal virtue. If we have a sense of humor, we should thank God for it. If we don't have it, we should go to work and cultivate it. A bad-tempered person is a humorless, juiceless person. Part of the trouble is that he takes himself too seriously, lacks any glimmering of fun when it is most needed, never looks in the mirror and laughs at himself. There is a lot of homely, practical wisdom in the saying of an old preacher, "If you could jist set on the fence and see yourself pass by, you'd die laughing at the sight." This is part of the appeal of the television program, *Candid Camera*.

> Oh wad some power the giftie gie us
> To see oursels as others see us.

A girl told her minister that her parents were not speaking to each other, and had not for some time. They were communicating, she said, by notes and by messages conveyed through the children. Believe it or not, the origin of the quarrel was whether a certain Mr. and Mrs. Jones should be invited to dinner. What a humorless, juiceless, jaundiced pair they must have been!

It makes us laugh even to think of them. But the girl, confiding in her minister, didn't find anything in the situation to laugh about. She was bewildered and becoming bitter. Sweet seventeen, with romance, courtship, love, marriage, a home and family of her own in mind, she was living under the same roof with a father and mother who were feuding, silent, sullen, sulky. This, quite literally, can be a destructive and deadly sin. Who can estimate with any adequacy the damage it does?

And to be wroth with one we love
Doth work like madness in the brain.

Anger, bad temper, resentment, hostility, can wreck the health of the body and the mind. They are as likely to cause disease as a germ. Psychiatrists write at length about illnesses brought about by mishandled emotions. Medical men warn their patients to keep anger in control and be on their guard against irritability and vindictiveness. Death from an apoplectic stroke is an everyday occurrence.

Nor is the damage suffered solely by the person whose anger gets out of control. Misery is created for others in countless ways. This is what leads to friction, starts disputes and demands for rights that are not worth bickering over, ends with regrets and remorse. This is what makes people a burden to their friends; first there is coolness and then estrangement. This is what makes some parents a terror to their children and a sore trial to their life's partner. Bad temper has been the beginning of the end of many a marriage. Things are said in anger that should never have been said—the marriage regretted, the marriage a disappointment, the marriage a mistake. Things are said that can never be unsaid, that linger and rankle in the memory for years, that cannot be wiped out by boxes of chocolates and dozens of roses, and may not be even by passionate tenderness and devotion.

Because anger does such damage it is not surprising to find moralists and the Bible urging us to bring it under strict control. There was an English bishop who said that the control of temper is nine-tenths of Christianity. John Wesley might have agreed with him, for he wrote: "I find more profit in sermons on either good tempers, or good works, than in what are vulgarly called Gospel sermons. That term has now become a mere cant word. I wish none of our society would use it. Let but a pert, self-sufficient animal, that has neither sense nor grace, bawl out something about Christ, or His blood, or justification by faith, and his hearers cry out: 'What a fine Gospel sermon!' "[2] Wesley and the bishop would have put great stress on the biblical injunction, "Let all bitterness, and wrath, and anger, and clamor, and evil speaking be put away from you, with all malice; and be ye kind one to another, tender-hearted, forgiving one another, even as God for Christ's sake has forgiven you." The latter part of that injunction I always read when officiating at a marriage. And in the interview preceding the marriage I draw attention to another biblical injunction, "Let not the sun go down upon your wrath." It is sound advice. If a misunderstanding arises, never carry it over to another day. Clear it up before the day is done, before it has time to fester. Keeping up a quarrel and the nursing of resentment blight marriage and make for the worst kind of misery. "Sulking is always bad; but between husband and wife it is damnable." One of the most engaging things about a child is the readiness with which he smiles and forgets.

To bring anger under strict control is an onerous undertaking. Some are born good-natured; they have an even, equable, contented —it may be bovine—disposition; it takes a lot to provoke them to wrath. Others have a prickly temper; it is a family characteristic; the son finds in himself the irritability he complains of in his father. A clergyman, rebuked for asperity, replied, "Young man, I control more temper every fifteen minutes than you will in your whole lifetime." The prickliness of the man shows in the defensive, self-justifying retort. Strenuous, sustained self-discipline is required to control anger. It is not enough to memorize maxims like "Count twenty before you speak" and "If the pot boils, take it off the fire." What is called for is the *sublimation* of these powerful emotions, their direction into channels that are constructive, not destructive. A Quaker, raged at by a merchant, received the outburst of ill-temper in silence. Afterward, ashamed of himself, the merchant asked the Quaker how he was able to maintain such self-control. "Friend," replied the other, "I will tell thee. I was naturally as hot and violent as thou art. I knew that to indulge temper was sinful, and I found it was imprudent. I observed that men in a passion always spoke loud, and I thought if I could control my voice I should suppress my passion. I have therefore made it a rule never to allow my voice to be above a certain key, and by a careful observance of this rule I have, by the blessing of God, mastered my natural temper."

By the blessing of God! People try to master temper on a do-it-yourself principle. They rely entirely on their own strength of will. Theirs is a "bootstrap religion." They are for all practical purposes atheists, without invisible supports. Yet sooner or later the discovery is forced on them that there are passions in them so strong and deep-rooted that they cannot get rid of them by their own volition. They have tried hard and for years to master anger and have failed. The direction the Bible gives is not "Be strong"—there is no Gospel in that; but "Be strong in the Lord and in the power of His might."

The way to self-control is through God-control. About this Paul is forthright: "Let not sin reign in your mortal bodies, to make you obey their passions. Do not yield your members to sin as instruments of wickedness, but yield yourselves to God as men who have been brought from death to life." What we cannot do by ourselves can be done with the help and by the blessing of God.

There is one consideration not to be overlooked. Anger is not always a sin. There are occasions when not to be angry is a sin. Tolerance or apathy in the presence of evil may mean that we are the victims of evil and even its instruments. There can be no spiritual life without moral indignation. "No heart is pure that is not passionate, no virtue is safe that is not enthusiastic." A good man is bound to be angry when he sees harm done to his brother man. "The size of a man can be measured by the size of the thing that makes him angry."

Dorothy Sayers had no patience with the conventional picture of Jesus as "a milk-and-water person," "certified as meek and mild," and "recommended as a fitting pet for pale curates and pious old ladies." Jesus was meek and gentle, but meek and gentle people are often the last people to trifle with. "He looked round on them with anger." "He was moved with indignation." What vehemence in the word used to describe Herod!—"Go and say to that fox. . . . " What wrath in the cleansing of the Temple! Where will we find invectives like those in Matthew: "hypocrites," "blind guides," "whitewashed sepulchres," "brood of vipers"? Obviously, anger at white heat, but never anger because of wrong done to Himself, always anger because of wrong done to God, because of man's inhumanity to man, always righteous anger. What we ought to ask ourselves is whether there is any of this kind of anger in us, whether we have ever been moved, as James Baldwin was moved when he wrote *Down at the Cross: Letter from a Region in My Mind*.[3] Are we instead smooth, suave, bland, urbane? One thing is certain: were moral indignation to die out of the world, society would swiftly rot to extinction.

Yet here also we have to be on our guard, have to be sure that our anger is righteous, our indignation moral. As the Bible has it, "Be angry *and sin not*." In denouncing the sins of others we can very readily lose sight of our own sins. We can "compound for sins we are inclined to, by damning those we have no mind to." There was the woman who said, "Anybody who tortures a helpless animal should be flogged till he shrieks for mercy." How little we know ourselves or the irrational tendencies at work in us! We all have cause to pray the prayer of George Matheson, "O Lord, Thou knowest that I do well to be angry, but I have mistaken the times."

The New Testament points the way to the best antidote for unrighteous anger. Henry Drummond said of the thirteenth chapter of First Corinthians that, read every day for six months, it would work a transformation in a person's disposition. "Love is patient and kind; love is not jealous or boastful; it is not arrogant or rude. Love does not insist on its own way; it is not irritable or resentful; it does not rejoice at wrong; but rejoices in the right. Love bears all things, believes all things, hopes all things, endures all things. Love never ends."

NOTES

[1] Author unknown.
[2] John Wesley, *Works* (Edit. 1872), Vol. XIII, p. 36.
[3] Part II of his *The Fire Next Time* (New York: Dial Press, 1962–63).

4. Sloth

THERE are many warnings against slothfulness in the Bible. Its writers have scant patience with the person who loafs his way through life, won't do a hand's turn, and doesn't lift a finger unless he has to. The admonition of the Book of Proverbs is typical: "Go to the ant, thou sluggard; consider her ways, and be wise." Paul in the New Testament is just as trenchant: "The man who will not work shall not eat." Then he adds, "We mention this because we hear that some of your number are idling their time away, minding everybody's business but their own."

On the positive side, there is an insistent emphasis in the Bible on the necessity, wholesomeness, and dignity of work. The Greeks said that manual labor was to be left to slaves; Aristotle's "perfect man" would not soil his hands with it. The Hebrews regarded work as a divine ordinance from which no one was exempted: "Six days shalt thou labor and do all thy work." (Do you hear of anybody nowadays taking the Decalogue literally and condemning the five-day week? The point is understood to be that an honest week's work is everybody's duty.) In New Testament times a rabbi had to learn a trade and support himself and his family; he was not allowed to receive payment for the performance of religious services. Paul was a tentmaker and Jesus was a carpenter. Not only so, but God was the Master-Worker. "And on the seventh day God finished his work which he had done, and he rested on the seventh day from all his work which he had done. So God blessed the seventh day and hallowed it, because on it God rested from all his labor which he had done." Work in the Bible is a necessary and honorable part of all life, human and divine.

Many of us were reared on a gospel of work. We were made to memorize "Satan finds some mischief still for idle hands to do," and, growing up in Scotland, I had to learn by rote Longfellow's *Psalm of Life,* with special emphasis given to the line: "Let us then be up and doing. . . ." An epitaph which a man wrote for himself, and which was intended to impress and, I think, solemnize us, had a

quite different effect. Psychological understanding of the mind of a
child has not always been perceptive. I quote the epitaph, and
leave it to the reader to judge what its effect on youthful teen-agers
was likely to be.

> He slept beneath the moon,
> He basked beneath the sun;
> He lived a life of going-to-do,
> And died with nothing done.

It was also impressed on us that laziness could be our undoing, that
for the slothful there would be no future, that we could not have
success without toiling for it, that there would be sharp competition
for life's glittering prizes and if we did not work, and work hard, we
would be pushed aside and before long would find ourselves out of
the running, mediocrities, nobodies. So we were told, the Bible
quoted to clinch matters, "Whatsoever thy hand findeth to do, do it
with all thy might."

Perhaps there is no country on earth where the gospel of work has
been given such enthusiastic advocacy as the United States. It was
extolled in Benjamin Franklin's *Poor Richard's Almanac* and in
the McGuffey Readers. It found an apostle in Henry Ford, who
wrote with the fervor of an evangelist: "There is no place in
civilization for the idler. None of us has any right to ease. Work is
our sanity, our self-respect, our salvation. Through work and work
alone may health, wealth and happiness inevitably be secured."
Ford would have maintained that idleness, not the love of money, is
the root of all evil, that industry is the highest virtue and poverty a
vice, a disgrace, the result of shiftlessness and indolence.

There have been dissenters to such sermonizing. One of the most
remarkable, some would say eccentric and odd, was Thoreau, a
contemporary, it should be remembered, of Horatio Alger and
Samuel Smiles. He refused to be hustled, to join the scramble for
the Almighty Dollar, and devoted himself to the life of contemplation. "The man," he wrote, "who does not betake himself at once
and desperately to sawing is called a loafer, though he may be
knocking at the doors of heaven all the while." Ever since I came
across a remark of Burton Rascoe I have treasured it, for it applies
to preachers as well as authors: "What no wife of a writer can ever
understand, no matter if she lives with him for twenty years, is that
a writer is working when he's staring out of the window."

Hard workers, a puritan strain inbred in them, have had a fear of leisure. They have even had a sense of guilt about pleasurable recreation. There was a time in New England when it was said that pleasures are like mushrooms, the wholesome so difficult to distinguish from the poisonous that it is better to abstain from them altogether. In the early days of the YMCA, *Punch,* the British periodical, was excluded from Association reading rooms because it was not sufficiently serious. Zealous secretaries of the Association, formulating a statement of policy, maintained: "It is no part of the YMCA to provide recreations or amusements for its members." Some went so far as to urge that "no Christian young man should take part in a swimming match, or indeed a match of any kind." Two prominent clergymen, Archbishop Trench and Dr. R. W. Dale, were rebuked for appearing at and sharing in the Shakespeare tercentenary celebrations at Stratford. In the deadly serious language of the time they were accused of "trailing their Christian priesthood in the dust by offering homage at the shrine of a dead playwright." What intense concentration on work and duty! What fear of leisure and pleasure! When Sir Walter Scott, as a child, said that he liked the soup, half a pint of cold water was poured into it.

Times have changed, and people have changed with them. There never was an age in which the prime necessities of life could be obtained with so little labor. As a consequence we are becoming enamored of soft living. We hustle more than our grandfathers did; the pace is faster; do we work as hard? The trend in America at the present time is in the direction of slackness and laxness. There is an inclination to put more emphasis on wages than on work. We can't or won't entertain ourselves; we have to be entertained. Many of us have a pitifully small stock of interests, ideas, emotions. We read fewer and fewer books and look at more and more television. Conversation is becoming a lost art because for nights on end families sit in silence, their eyes riveted on a television screen. It is a fact that we have more leisure at our disposal than any preceding generation. A thirty-five-hour working week is now common. Subtract the hours worked in the week from 168, the total number; what do we do with the remainder? Have we ever sat down and made an accounting of the way in which we spend our time? I press the question because, unless we wake up to what is happening, the hours can be frittered away aimlessly, selfishly, trivially. Triviality —its first cousin banality—is one of the besetting sins of our society, and never far from either is that archenemy of human happiness, boredom.

These three, triviality, banality, and boredom, taken together, bring us close to what was in the thinking of the preachers of the Middle Ages when they included sloth among the seven deadly sins. The word they used to lay bare the nature of this particular sin many have never heard of. It does not appear in some dictionaries, though it is to be found in Webster. It has all but gone out of vogue, yet the thing is still rife. The word is *acedia,* and it stands for the devitalizing of our energies, physical, mental, and spiritual, which is the price that has to be paid for indolence and laziness. If we give way to sloth, we are soon in the grip of apathy. If we adopt the "I can't be bothered" attitude, before long our attitude will be "I couldn't care less." This is true at the physical level in the matter of exercise, at the mental level in the matter of books and serious reflection, at the spiritual level in the matter of the practice of the presence of God.

> Life is not lost by dying! Life is lost
> Minute by minute, day by dragging day,
> In all the thousand, small uncaring ways.
> And millions now living are dead.[1]

Acedia, torpor leading to apathy, is a deadly sin. Anger slays its thousands, acedia its tens of thousands. Where we have an affluent society we are certain to find it—abundance, then satiety, then torpor, then apathy. And when apathy is widespread people are heard saying, "So what?" "Oh, yeah!" "Aw, what the heck!" "I don't give a damn." When apathy has its grip on a man he "believes in nothing, cares for nothing, seeks to know nothing, interferes with nothing, enjoys nothing, loves nothing, hates nothing, finds purpose in nothing, lives for nothing, and only remains alive because there is nothing he would die for." The end result of apathy is "the blues." To cure "the blues" many turn, not to work or social service or a religious faith, but to drink, dope, tranquilizers, sex, gambling, a round of frivolous amusement, which aggravates their condition so that their last state is worse than their first. Sloth is a common sin and a deadly one.

How is it to be dealt with? Unlike anger it cannot be sublimated and directed into useful channels. The only way to conquer it is to be rid of it. Work will do it, good, hard, honest work, the work by which we earn our living, the worthwhile use we make of our leisure. But work must have a purpose, a motive. Despite the endless, wearisome urging of television commercials, disinclination to work is not due simply to lack of vitamins. There are people who dose themselves with vitamins; who are robust physically, but mentally and spiritually in a state of torpor. To work well, hard, and honestly we must have a faith, something we care about, something we really believe in, something that inspires a sense of mission, something that gives life high meaning and sacred significance. A friend wrote to Turgenev: "It seems to me that to put oneself in the second place is the whole significance of life." Turgenev's answer was: "It seems to me that to discover what to put before oneself, in the first place, is the whole problem of life." For money some work hard. For their family some work hard. For their country some work hard. For God some work hard. When God is at the center of a person's life he is conscious of what Whitehead calls "eternal greatness in the passage of time," and he has found the cure for the torpor that leads to apathy.

I have written about people who to be rid of "the blues" resort to drink, dope, tranquilizers, sex, gambling, a round of frivolous amusement. For those of us who are nonaddicts the reference may itself be a tranquilizer. Focussing attention on the problems of others may take our minds off our own problems. We may not be troubled by physical torpor; there may not be a lazy bone in our bodies. We may not be troubled by mental torpor; the edges of our minds may be as keen as the blade of a razor. What about spiritual torpor, the torpor that leads to apathy of soul? How is it with our souls? We are not slothful in business; are we slothful in the saying of our prayers, in the worship and service of God? Do we labor for more than the meat which perishes? This is where practically all of us are vulnerable. "It is high time for us to awake out of sleep."

One Sunday Dr. Alexander Whyte went into the pulpit of Free St. George's Church, Edinburgh, and said: "I often wonder as I go on working among you, if you ever attach any meaning or make any application to yourselves of all those commands and counsels of which the Scriptures are full—to be up and doing, to watch and pray, to watch and be sober, to fight the good fight of faith, to hold the fort, to rise early, and even by night, and to endure unto death, and never for one moment to be found off your guard. Do you attach any real meaning to these examples of the psalmists, to these continued commands and examples of Christ? Do you? Against whom and against what do you fight? What fort do you hold?"[2]

The example of Christ! "I must work," He said, "while it is day; the night cometh when no man can work." "My meat is to do the will of him who sent me and to accomplish his work." No sloth there, no torpor, no apathy—and no blues. Christ had a spirit as fresh as a spring. "The water that I shall give," He said, "will be an inner spring always welling up for eternal life." "He has left us an example that we should follow in His steps."

NOTES

[1] "A Child Is Born," from *We Stand United and Other Radio Scripts* by Stephen Vincent Benét, published by Holt, Rinehart and Winston, Inc., 1945. Reprinted by permission of Brandt & Brandt.

[2] Alexander Whyte, *Bunyan Characters in The Pilgrim's Progress,* second series (London: Oliphants, Ltd.), pp. 116–17.

5. Avarice

AVARICE is by universal consent a horrid, ugly thing. Self-knowledge being rare, we may not see it in ourselves, but when it comes to the surface in others we don't like what we see. Let us be quite sure that we understand what it is. It is not the desire for money, property, prestige, power. There is nothing evil in any of those in and by themselves. People say, "Money is the root of all evil," and think they are quoting Scripture. They are misquoting Scripture. "The love of money is the root of all evil": the excessive, unbridled desire for it, the greedy, grasping, ruthless determination to get it—to get it no matter at what cost to others and to oneself—to get it with no thought of sharing it, to get and hoard it. The same thing is true of the excessive, unbridled passion for possessions, status, authority.

Avarice is an ugly sin and it makes people ugly. Was there ever a miser with an open countenance? Was there ever a hustling huckster whose face didn't tell sooner or later what he had been up to? Time and again, the face is the index of the soul. What must the soul of a skinflint, a moneygrubber, be like? No need there to pose, pretend, dissemble. Some sins—sins of the body we call them to distinguish them from sins of the disposition—are passionate and warmhearted, sins like gluttony and lust. There is nothing warmhearted about avarice. It is calculating and cold.

> But och! it hardens a' within,
> And petrifies the feeling!

Avarice! Note its last three letters—*ice*. In etymological origin, the word miser denotes a person who is miserable. It would never occur to an artist to portray an avaricious person with a spring in his step or a smile on his face. We know what did occur to T. S. Eliot in the poem he wrote about our affluent society that has for its ironical title, "A Penny for the Old Guy." "We are the hollow men. We are the stuffed men. . . ." Why is avarice a deadly sin? It isn't enough to say that it is ugly and harmful and leads to unhappiness. Let it begin to dominate a man and it will finally destroy him—ice in the heart, ulcers in the stomach, penury in the soul. "You fool, this night your soul will be required of you; you have made your money—who will get it now?"

David Hume in an essay on this subject tells a grim story.

A miser, being dead and fairly interred, comes to the banks of the Styx desiring to be ferried over along with the other ghosts. Charon demands his fare, and is surprised to see the miser, rather than pay it, throw himself into the river and swim to the other side, notwithstanding all the clamor and opposition that could be made to him. All hell was in an uproar; and each of the judges was meditating some punishment suitable to a crime of such dangerous consequence to the infernal revenues. Shall he be chained to the rock with Prometheus, or tremble below the precipice in company with the Danaïdes? No, says Mynos, none of these. We must invent some severer punishment. Let him be sent back to earth to see the use his heirs are making of his riches.[1]

The mention of misers and hucksters may leave us feeling uninvolved and mentally at ease. Not only so, we may be unsparing in our condemnation of them. But, if we turn a searchlight in upon ourselves, we won't get off so easily and lightly. If there is one thing more than another that is impressive about a study of the seven deadly sins it is that nobody is completely free from any of them. To admit this hurts our self-esteem. We rally at once to our defense, all our self-justifying impulses at work, but do we not rationalize rather than reason, evade facts rather than face them? Avarice is a case in point. Have we no acquisitiveness in our nature, none at all? Is there not a trace of covetousness in us? Have we no inordinate desires, not a single one? Can we truthfully say that we have never craved money but have always, at every stage of our life, put spiritual values above pecuniary considerations? The person who, with those questions a test, scores a hundred is a paragon; the only course open to the rest of us is to say what Moses did when he was at the back of the desert and saw the burning bush: "I will turn aside, and see this great sight."

Avarice is not a sin to which only the rich are prone. It is extraordinary that when a certain type of man has an abundance of this world's goods he should go on feverishly adding to his store. The more he gets the more he seems to want to get. Long after his children and grandchildren are handsomely provided for he is still hard at the business of amassing what he is pleased to call securities. People of modest means, however, can be avaricious too. Thrift is a

virtue that can be carried to the place where it becomes a vice. At
the other extreme from prodigality is niggardliness, and niggardliness is a frightfully narrowing force. I think of a man known to me
who hoarded money, refused to spend it on the education of his
children, dressed shabbily, ate sparingly, denied himself travel,
holidays, little luxuries. To begin with he may have been safeguarding himself and his family against a rainy day, but in time that
contingency was reasonably covered. He went on hoarding, and he
shrivelled up with every passing year. He was a penny pincher and
had no need to be one. Avarice has inconspicuous as well as
conspicuous victims.

Greed for money is not the only way avarice shows itself. Remember what it is—excessive, unbridled desire. Some who have no
hankering after money, and realize that they are never likely to
have much of it, crave kudos. This, they say, is the besetting sin of
preachers—the temptation to shine, to be in the limelight, to court
publicity, to be well thought of. "They love the uppermost rooms at
feasts, and the chief seats in the synagogues, and to be called
'Doctor' by their fellows"—it was about the clergy our Lord said
that.

Some who have no hankering after money crave authority. The
greed for it is often stronger than the greed for money. If money is
sought, it is chiefly for what it can do, for the weight it is then
possible to throw around. "I say to one, 'Go,' and he goes, and to
another, 'Come,' and he comes, and to my subordinate, 'Do this,'
and he does it."

> But man, proud man
> Drest in a little brief authority,
> Most ignorant of what he's most assured,
> His glassy essence, like an angry ape,
> Plays such fantastic tricks before high heaven
> As makes the angels weep.[2]

Scarcely a day passes but we see it—parents with children, teachers
with pupils, employers with employees, policemen as they direct
traffic, magnifying their office. Can it be that we have never caught
a glimpse of it in ourselves?

Avarice and covetousness are all but indistinguishable, and the
Bible is blunt about the sin of coveting: coveting another man's
wife—the New Testament repeatedly links covetousness with lust
and sex; coveting another man's property—his house, automobile,

club memberships. To see covetousness stripped and naked, look once—only once—at the television show, *The Price Is Right*.

Christians should be at pains to avoid censoriousness and smug complacency, because the Church, while always roundly condemning avarice, does not herself have a spotless record. There is a scorching passage in Dorothy Sayers' book, *Creed or Chaos?* (To think that it was left to a woman to lift up her voice when the clergy should have been the first to speak up and out!)

The Church says Covetousness is a deadly sin—but does she really think so? Is she ready to found Welfare Societies to deal with financial immorality as she does with sexual immorality? Do the officials stationed at church doors in Italy to exclude women with bare arms turn anybody away on the grounds that they are too well-dressed to be honest? Do the vigilance committees who complain of "suggestive" books and plays make any attempt to suppress the literature which "suggests" that getting on in the world is the chief end in life? Is Dives, like Magdalen, ever refused the sacraments on the grounds that he, like her, is an "open and notorious evil-liver"? Does the Church arrange services with bright congregational singing, for Total Abstainers from Usury?[3]

There can be no question where Dorothy Sayers learned that language. It was from Him who said, "What will it profit a man, if he gains the whole world and loses his own soul?" It was from Him who said, "Take heed, and beware of all covetousness; for a man's life does not consist in the abundance of his possessions." Jesus warned men and women against avarice. He warned them against money as dangerous and deceitful, as a manifold source of injustice and cruelty, as a foe to the life of the spirit. What did His hearers make of pronouncements like these? "Blessed are you poor! The kingdom of God is yours." "Woe to you rich folk! You get all the comforts you will ever get." "How hard it is for the wealthy to enter the kingdom of God! It is easier for a camel to go through the eye of a needle than for a rich man to enter the kingdom of God." What do we make of them? Do we find it as hard to get *round* the needle's eye as a camel would find it to get *through?* Jesus challenged currently accepted standards of value. He saw that money was grossly overvalued, and not by the rich alone. He denounced those who came by it dishonestly, spent it selfishly, relied on it as the supreme good. He saw the acquisitive instinct as a threat to the soul. He saw weak men who had been corrupted by money and who had become sensualists. He saw strong men who had been hardened by money and who had become predatory and piratical. He bids us be on our guard against the deadly sin of avarice.

From Jesus we learn best how this sin is overcome. He sees it in all of us, so readily stirred, taking so many forms, appearing in so many disguises, so ingrained as to seem ineradicable. Some believe that its hold is so tenacious and subtle that it can never be completely eliminated. Jesus shows in His teaching, in His life and His death, how it can be subdued and vanquished. He offers us more than the maxims of moralists, more than an ideal. An ideal can be a frustration. We try, try repeatedly to live up to it, and falling short over and over again, despair both of our efforts and of ourselves. Jesus awakens us to the higher values, inclines us toward them, wins our devotion to them. We learn from Him that the cure for avarice does not consist in desiring less but in desiring more, in desiring wholeheartedly what really matters. It consists in love of the priorities, the things money cannot buy. It consists in the love of God and of our neighbor, which frees us from the itch for aggrandizement, status, superiority, authority—the love that "envieth not, vaunteth not itself, seeketh not its own." Jesus brings to us "the expulsive power of a new affection." He brings fulfilment of the ancient promise, "A new heart will I give you, and a new spirit will I put within you."

There was no trace of avarice in Him, no grain of cupidity, nothing grasping or greedy. In life and in death He provided the supreme example of love of the enduring values. He sought first the Kingdom of God and His righteousness. His meat was to do the will of Him who sent Him and to accomplish His work. The end for which He came into the world and went, bearing His cross to Calvary, was to redeem us from self-seeking, to reveal to us the infinite love of God, and to kindle the flame of that love in our hearts. The only sure way to keep clear of avarice is to keep close to Him. How does one keep close to Him? There are four books, Matthew, Mark, Luke, and John. Read them. Steep your mind in them. Get to know them better than you know any book that has ever been written. That is the way to keep close to Him.

NOTES

[1] David Hume, "Essay on Avarice."

[2] Shakespeare, *Measure for Measure*, Act II, Sc. 2.

[3] Dorothy Sayers, *Creed or Chaos?* (New York: Harcourt, Brace & Co., 1949), p. 73.

6. Gluttony

"WHOSE end is destruction, whose god is their belly, and whose glory is in their shame, who mind earthly things." So runs the King James Version of Paul's judgment on gluttons. The language is plain, blunt, outspoken, too much so for some today. Modern versions of the Bible tend to tone it down, J. B. Phillips, for instance, offering this rendering: "Their god is their own appetite; their pride is in what they should be ashamed of; and this world is the limit of their horizon." The paraphrase gets at Paul's meaning but the translators of King James' day, it seems to me, were closer to his mind. He was describing something gross and was not troubled by squeamishness in denouncing it.

From the earliest times the Church singled out gluttony as a deadly sin. There is no question that in century after century it has been a besetting temptation for many. St. Thomas Aquinas in his generation was at pains, and felt he had to be, in defining and detailing wherein gluttony was a sin. It consisted in eating too soon, eating at the wrong time, having no patience to wait, no will power to fast, no self-discipline. It consisted in eating too much, in giving in to a voracious appetite, an intemperate desire for food and drink. It consisted in eating too fast, too eagerly, too greedily, in making a pig of oneself. It consisted in eating too expensively, in doting on fine and rare foods. St. Thomas distinguished between the gourmand whose one thought is for quantity and the gourmet whose one thought is for quality, but he held that both are at fault. Connoisseurs in eating and drinking will disagree with his condemnation of the gourmet. The contention of St. Thomas was that to be finicky and fussy over the preparation of food, the way it is cooked, seasoned, served, to make of appetite a cult, is to be a glutton.

Books of social history, European and American, tell an extraordinary story in this connection—breakfasts in the case of the wealthy that were gargantuan meals, banquets lasting for three hours where prodigious quantities of food were consumed, country mansions built with peeping galleries about the dining hall to which ladies might retire and watch to see whose husband was last under the table. Trevelyan's *English Social History* provides an account of a typical "elegant" dinner. "The first course was, part of a large cod, a chine of mutton, some soup, a chicken pie, pudding and roots etc. Second course, pigeons and asparagus, a fillet of veal with mushrooms and high sauce with it, roasted sweetbreads, hot lobster, apricot tart and in the middle a pyramid of syllabubs and jellies. We had a dessert of fruit after dinner, and Madeira, white Port and red to drink as wine. We were all very cheerful and merry."[1] But while the privileged class overindulged and gorged itself the poor could not pay the price of a loaf of bread, were wretchedly housed and clothed, and frequently close to starvation. Did chaplains of the privileged class ever preach from the text, "Whose end is destruction, whose god is their belly, and whose glory is in their shame, who mind earthly things"?

Isn't all this, however, a thing of the past? To a considerable degree, Yes. We are not the trenchermen, the voracious eaters and insatiable guzzlers, that some of our ancestors were. On the contrary, more and more people in our day are weight-conscious, are calory-conscious, are preoccupied with diet charts and reducing charts so that they may keep themselves slim and trim. St. Francis of Assisi playfully referred to his body as Brother Ass. He was never in any doubt that it was meant to be the dutiful servant of the mind and the spirit. On the other hand, ours is an age that makes a cult of the body. Marilyn Monroe, when all is said and done, was a symbol, a pathetic symbol. Think of the attention concentrated on the body in advertisements, novels, plays. Contrast with the money lavished on food, clothes, medicines, cosmetics what people will spend for the cultivation of their minds. If Paul were among us today and describing our affluent society, might he not say, "Whose god is their body, whose glory [because of the exaggerated emphasis placed on sex] is in their shame, who mind earthly things"?

Gluttony even in its gross form has not disappeared. There are still people in plenty who live to eat rather than eat to live, who stuff themselves with food, drink cocktail after cocktail, smoke like chimneys. A doctor in a restaurant drew the attention of a friend to a corpulent man avidly writing an order check from a menu. "Look," he said, "there is a man writing his autobiography from a menu card." The judgment may strike us as harsh, but basically it was sound. In a book with the title *Physiologie du Goût* there is a

sentence, "Tell me what you eat, and I will tell you what you are."
A widow, asked by associates of her husband what ought to be
carved on his gravestone, replied: "I think a carving of a quarter-
inch porterhouse steak would do very well. That seemed to be the
thing he got most excited about." A woman said at table to her
guest, "May I give you some more?" The answer she got was, "Yes,
thank you. Pork always makes me ill, but I am so fond of it I really
can't say No."

Gluttony is not simply a matter of stuffing oneself with food.
Nowadays there are people who are sparing in what they eat, but it
cannot be said that they are as self-disciplined in regard to what
they drink. Cocktails at lunch, cocktails at social functions in the
afternoon, cocktails before dinner—extraordinary quantities of
liquor consumed, and in many cases no thought given to moderation, temperance, not to speak of gluttony. The rule seems to be
"Everybody's doing it, why shouldn't I?"—whereas it might well be
"Everybody's doing it, why should I?" Consider the statement of Dr.
Marvin A. Block, an official of the American Medical Association,
made to the National Council on Alcoholism. "There is need of a
council on alcoholism; it is estimated that in the United States
alcoholics are increasing at the rate of upwards of 50,000 a year, and
'problem drinkers' (those who have three bracers a day) at the rate
of 200,000 a year." Dr. Block argued that the public needs a
thorough revision of its entire book of etiquette at every point
where it touches on the matter of social drinking. He pointed out
that the necessity for drinking in American culture has become so
widespread that "the individual who does not drink often feels
himself conspicuous or, worse, sometimes ostracized." He went on,
"It is a sad commentary on the depth of our interest in each other
that no group can successfully get through a party without the
gurgle and splash of alcoholic drinks." Then he asked, "Would it
not be better to encourage respect for those who can be interesting
without drinking?"[2]

If we bear in mind what gluttony is, that the essence of it is
intemperate desire, it will be obvious that a case can be made about
excess in smoking as well as in eating and drinking. Take the chain
smoker and the torment he is in when he cannot get his hand on a
cigarette. Everyone is now familiar with the pronouncements of
medical experts relating the danger of cancer to cigarette smoking.
Even were there no such danger, when the habit becomes compul-
sive the situation should surely be taken in hand. If a desire

becomes overmastering and is yielded to without even a show of resistance, control is lost, or in the language of the Bible, the spirit is subordinated to the flesh. Gluttony is not an attractive word yet it is the word to apply in such a case. I wonder if in universities today there are professors saying anything like what Sir William Osler said to students at Yale half a century ago: "A bitter enemy to the bright eye and the clear brain of the early morning is tobacco when smoked to excess, as it is now by a large majority of students. Watch it, test it, and if need be, control it. That befogged woolly sensation reaching from the forehead to the occiput, that haziness of memory, that cold fishlike eye, that furred tongue and last week's taste in the mouth—too many of you know them—I know them—they often come from too much tobacco."[3] With that, match the drivel heard on television about soothing, relaxing, refreshing filter cigarettes.

Something should be written also about the immoderate and gluttonous desire for things—commodities, goods, luxuries. We have a problem in this country with overproduction. Is the only solution of the problem increased consumption, with an interminable barrage of advertisements designed to stimulate that end? "Buy now—the job you save may be your own." "Buy and be happy." "Buy—it's your patriotic duty." "Buy your way to prosperity." Herbert Hoover held out the prospect of a day when there would be two chickens in every pot. That is modest, Quakerish, compared with current slogans. The Douglas Fir Plywood Association says every family needs two homes. Detroit says every family needs two cars. A spokesman for Revlon claims that it has taught women to match their nail enamel to their moods and occasions, so that they buy more. What can the peoples of Africa and Asia feel about what must seem to them sheer extravagance? Is waste no longer wicked? Is thrift no longer a virtue? Can there be high thinking without plain living? There is a great deal of talk about consumption catching up with production. Why isn't more said about distribution, equitable distribution? What others feel about us comes out in this comment from Europe: "A society in which consumption has to be artificially stimulated in order to keep production going is a society founded on trash and waste, and such a society is a house built upon sand."

In all this it may seem that I am advocating stringent asceticism. I am not, but I do urge this: a strain of asceticism in our national life would help to toughen our moral fiber. Bear in mind, however, that Christianity is not in the strict sense of the term an ascetic religion. It does not denounce pleasure as sinful simply because it is pleasurable. The instincts and appetites are not evil in themselves; it is when they are abused that evil is done. Taste is one of the five God-given senses. The person who says he does not care what he eats, though he may say it with pride, is a person with a sad deficiency. He should ask himself whether he would be proud of being dull of hearing, or shortsighted, or devoid of the sense of smell and the sense of touch. Why should taste be thought a lower sense than the other four? A fine palate is as much the gift of God as an eye that discerns beauty and an ear that appreciates music. "Every man," says the Bible, "should eat and drink and enjoy the fruit of his labor; it is the gift of God." What Christianity condemns is excessive indulgence, indulgence as in the case of the epicure made an end in itself, indulgence at the expense of others, indulgence that is self-destructive and deadly because it is injurious to the health of the body and ruinous to the health of the soul.

Mahatma Gandhi once said, "I eat to live, to serve, and also, if it so happens to enjoy, but I do not eat for the sake of enjoyment." That is asceticism. Christianity when it is true to the New Testament neither teaches nor requires asceticism. How could it? "The Son of Man came eating and drinking." His enemies called Him a glutton and a tippler. The charge was sheer fabrication, was downright libel. What were the facts? He was no "pale Galilean." The world did not "grow grey" at His breath. He not only entered into the sorrows of men and women but into their joys as well. He was not an ascetic like John the Baptist. He was in His element at a wedding and often at dinner parties. "I have come," He said, "that you might have life, and have it abundantly." But for Christ the body was the junior partner in the house of life, and the senior partner was the soul. They were not opposed the one to the other; the well-being of the one contributed to the well-being of the other; but there was never any doubt about the priority of the soul. "Seek first the kingdom of God." "What shall it profit a man if he shall gain the whole world and lose his own soul?"

This is where all of us stand condemned. We are so solicitous about the body and so neglectful of the soul. What do we make of the affirmation of the New Testament? "Your body is the temple of the Holy Spirit." The physical the shrine of the spiritual! The inner life the center of all that is divinest in us! How is it with our soul?

NOTES

[1] George M. Trevelyan, *English Social History* (London: Longmans, Green and Co., 1942), p. 409.

[2] *New York Times,* April 20, 1963, p. 11.

[3] William Osler, *A Way of Life* (London: Constable and Co., n.d.), p. 27.

7. Lust

LUST is a cardinal sin from which nobody is altogether free. We are all potentially lustful, and a huge proportion of us are so in thought if not in deed. If the generalization seems too sweeping, recall what Jesus said to a group of men who prided themselves on their puritanism and would have imposed the death penalty for adultery: "He that is without sin among you, let him first cast a stone at her." They slipped away, the record has it, "one by one, beginning at the eldest, even unto the last."

At one time the word lust stood for excessive desire of any kind, for food, drink, pleasure, money. This is the sense in which it is used in the King James Version of the Bible. In our time the word is mostly understood as referring to one type of desire, sexual desire. Something of the same sort has happened to the word immorality. It should cover wrongdoing in all its aspects; instead, it is associated almost exclusively with sexual sin. The point, to quote from her once again, is put incisively by Dorothy Sayers.

Perhaps the bitterest commentary of the way in which Christian doctrine has been taught in the last few centuries is the fact that to the majority of people the word "immorality" has come to mean one thing and one thing only. The name of an association like yours [she was addressing a Church of England Moral Welfare Society] is generally held to imply that you are concerned to correct only one sin out of those seven which the Church recognizes as capital. By a hideous irony, our shrinking reprobation of that sin has made us too delicate so much as to name it, so that we have come to use for it the words which were made to cover the whole range of human corruption. A man may be greedy and selfish; spiteful, cruel, jealous, and unjust; violent and brutal; grasping, unscrupulous, and a liar; stubborn and arrogant; stupid, morose, and dead to every noble instinct—and still we are ready to say of him that he is not an immoral man. I am reminded of a young man who once said to me with perfect simplicity: "I did not know that there were seven deadly sins: please tell me the names of the other six."[1]

For centuries the Church showed a tendency to identify sexuality and lust. The fact is that it spoke with two voices. On the one hand, it repeatedly made strong pronouncements on the sanctity of sex and marriage, while on the other hand there were Church Fathers who extolled and exalted celibacy and spoke of sex as though it were unclean. It is impossible to estimate the harm that was done by the latter teaching. The idea that sex in itself is sinful, that it is vulgar, smutty, obscene, took wide hold and surrounded the whole subject with embarrassment, shame, and guilt. To this day, though it is among the most powerful of our instincts, comparatively little is said about it in churches, and when something is said there are those who deplore the mention of it and would rather have the pulpit observe a rule of silence.

The churches for the most part may be silent; the other agencies in society shaping public opinion are not. Our grandparents may have shrouded the subject in furtive secrecy, but today it is right out in the open. The whole atmosphere of modern life is drenched and saturated with sex. Because it may be thought that a minister of the Christian religion, subconsciously still under the influence of the teaching of the Church Fathers, takes a jaundiced view of the matter, I cite a comment made by the novelist and playwright J. B. Priestley, who says that he has no religion, that most of his friends have none, that very few modern writers have any. Dealing with the point that literature is doing what it can to help in solving the mammoth problems of our day, he states flatly that it cannot carry the load and criticizes its obsession with sex. "Since the Second War, in this atomic age, sure of nothing but sex—and, to take two successful English examples, what is there left at the end of *Lucky Jim* or *Look Back in Anger* but sex?—we are now piling on to sex the whole gigantic load of our increasing dissatisfactions, our despair, a burden far greater than it can safely take."[2]

Mr. Priestley may not be religious, but his is the concern of many who are. Their protest is not against sex as such but against what is being made of it, the exaggerated emphasis given to it, the extent to which it has become an obsession, the way in which it is being exploited, the people who are keeping the sex instinct inflamed in order to make money, Elizabeth Taylor receiving upward of $7,000,000 for her *Cleopatra!* What can Africans, Asians, and the Soviets be making of that senseless extravagance and folly? A society in which it is possible already has in it the seeds of rottenness and decay.

The protest, it needs to be re-emphasized, is not against sex as such. Sex is sacred, not sinful. What is sacred can never be promiscuous, but this is not to say that prudery and Christianity are virtually synonymous. The Bible begins with the story of creation, and included in creation is the fact of sexuality. The Bible does not teach that the body is a prison house of sensuality from which we must seek to escape. On the contrary, it teaches that the body has a sacramental function whereby the relationship between a husband and wife becomes a union and communion of self-giving and mutual enrichment. "God," the Book of Genesis says, "created man and woman in his own image . . . male and female he created them." "From the beginning of creation," Jesus says, "God made them male and female. For this reason a man shall leave his father and mother and be joined to his wife, and the two shall become one. So they are no longer two but one. What therefore God has joined together, let not man put asunder." With both passages in mind, William Temple, Archbishop of Canterbury, wrote: "It is to be recognized that sex is holy as well as wholesome. . . . Any one who has once understood that, will be quite as careful as any Puritan to avoid making jokes about sex; not because it is nasty but because it is sacred. He would no more joke about sex than he would about Holy Communion—and for exactly the same reason. To joke about it is to treat with lightness something that deserves reverence."[3]

What must be protested is the common tendency to make sex an end in itself and to give it a priority to which it has no claim. It then becomes a cult, an egocentric cult, with personal gratification the overriding consideration, with people in self-justification talking about their need of fulfillment and their right to happiness, yet often oblivious of the rights and happiness of others, of a marriage partner and of children. All is in the name of love, but what sort of love is it that flouts duty and obligation, honor and fidelity, and dismisses sex taboos, the Ten Commandments, and Christian standards of morality as puritanical, obscurantist, and outmoded?

Sex, made an end in itself, is confused with and misrepresented as love. Sometimes it drives out and usurps the place of love. Sometimes sex is loveless—it *uses* the other person, regards him or her as means more than end, as a thing. The Don Juan type is a poor specimen of a man. He is a moral vagrant, and his female counterpart as often as not a tramp. The worst evil in fornication and prostitution is not the gratification, not the surrender of self-control, not the possibility of venereal disease, but the terrible impersonality, each treating the other as an object of desire; in the case of the prostitute, professional or amateur, as a means of gain.

We are being told a pack of thundering lies nowadays about sex. In its biologic aspect, romanticized and glamorized, it is mistaken for love. There is high-sounding talk about the evil of repression, the need of self-enrichment, the right to happiness. But love in its essence is self-transcendence. Love puts far more stress on giving than on receiving. At the root of many marital troubles and difficulties is self-absorption, self-indulgence. Marriage is increasingly regarded as a pleasurable, perhaps experimental venture, which carries with it no binding, lifelong obligations. "If it doesn't work out," the saying goes, "we can always have another try." Lost sight of is the fact that love is moral and spiritual as well as physical. D. H. Lawrence called the attachment based on no more than physical attraction counterfeit love, and had this to say about it. "A young couple fall in counterfeit love and fool themselves and each other completely. Alas, counterfeit love is good cake but bad bread. It produces a fearful emotional indigestion. Then you get a modern marriage, and a still more modern separation." In periodicals, plays, and novels, at the theater and on television, we are told that sex has priority right and may be put before everything else. It is a lie. In many of the richest, fullest, most vivid lives sex has played a subordinate part. In all the best lives it is disciplined and controlled, is servant, not master.

One is reminded of the question put to Calvin Coolidge when he got home from church: "What was the sermon about?" "Sin." "What stand did the preacher take?" "Against." Where sexual laxity is concerned, condemnation and denunciation will accomplish nothing. Noteworthy in this connection are the Monday issues of newspapers and their reports of pulpit utterances. The descriptive verbs again and again are "chides," "scores," "hits," "blasts," and not unnaturally the impression is abroad that churches and Christians major most of the time in censure. Merely to pass strictures on moral laxity is worse than useless. We have to uncover symptoms and point to cures rather than engage in verbal vituperation, to get at root causes and inner motivations with a view to accounting for the fact that our society is so saturated with sex. Isn't it in the final analysis because of inner emptiness? It is a powerful evidence of the imperative need of every human being to find meaning and satisfaction in life. People turn to lust because of ennui, boredom, dissatisfaction, their inability to make constructive use of leisure. From it they hope for excitement, adventure, or in the case of the middle-aged, one last fling! It is resorted to as an antidote to the flatness of existence, a means of filling the vacuum in their inner life. From churches and Christians it is not denunciation that is called for but sympathetic understanding and exemplification in character and conduct of the faith which provides life with high meaning and enduring satisfaction.

Jesus was the "friend of publicans and sinners," that is, of the immoral in the sense the majority understand the word. He said that He had expressly come to seek and save them. He spent hours of time in their company, trying to lure them to higher levels of life, making the spiritual world real and radiant. He was severe in His judgment on sins of the disposition and compassionate toward men and women guilty of what have been called the warmhearted sins. But He never condoned them. "Where are your accusers?" He asked the woman taken in adultery. "Has no man condemned you?" "No man, Lord," she replied. "Neither do I condemn you," He said, and added, "Go, and *sin no more.*" Moral laxity cannot be attributed to Jesus. Marriage with complete faithfulness to one's partner is His principle, and like all His principles it is stringent and exacting. It is the most unpopular of all His principles. Many say they are not Christians because they do not understand Him. Many, many more are not Christians because they understand Him only too well. Which is the more difficult, the personal ethic of Jesus or His social ethic? Either way, it is hard to be a Christian. Jesus knew that. He said that the big battalions would never be gathered before the narrow gate. But in this case narrowness does not mean that life is bleached of color and robbed of lasting joys and solid pleasures. He Himself was the happiest of persons, though no stranger to sorrow, and for Him life was full of zest and meaning. And the zest, the high meaning, all His true followers know. Did He not say "I have come that you might have life, and have it abundantly"?

NOTES

1 Dorothy Sayers, *Creed or Chaos* (New York: Harcourt, Brace & Co., 1949), p. 63.

2 J. B. Priestley, *Literature and Western Man* (New York: Harper & Brothers, 1960), p. 444.

3 William Temple, *Christian Faith and Life* (New York: The Macmillan Co., 1931), p. 49.

The Seven Cardinal Virtues

I do not speak much of vice, which is far the more easy theme, because I am entirely taken up with the abundance of worth and beauty in virtue, and have so much to say of the positive and intrinsic goodness of its nature. But besides, since a straight line is the measure both of itself and of a crooked one, I conclude that the very glory of virtue, well understood, will make all vice appear like dirt before a jewel.

—Thomas Traherne

1. Wisdom

WISDOM is customarily accorded pride of place among the cardinal virtues. In essence it is moral insight. If we have it we are capable of a true discrimination of values; we have an understanding of what is most worth living for; to the degree that we have it, we have mastered the art of living. In the Parable of the Rich Farmer, Jesus has God call the man a fool. By fool is meant not that he was stupid or asinine; he must have been smart and sharp to have succeeded so well. What is meant is that his sense of values, his scale of values was foolish, was absurdly out of proportion. This applies no less to society than to individuals. A nation is wise if it has moral insight, if it has a sound grasp of values and understands what it ought for the public good to aim at and strive after and put first.

Here is one of the deepest needs of our civilization. And the more we think about wisdom the more we appreciate that it is not a commodity that can be produced on demand. There is force in the biblical saying that it cannot be purchased with gold or silver. We have wealth, education, a control of our environment that would have left Plato and Aristotle gaping, but along with them a dearth of wisdom and a desperate confusion of values. We attach great importance to intellectual understanding and emotional satisfaction, though a lot of people find emotional satisfaction in the strangest quarters. What a fuss has been made over the Beatles, surely Britain's weirdest export in many, many moons! Where we are deficient is in moral insight, the perception of true values, the ability to face the practical problems of existence, personal and social, and work our way through to their solution. Wisdom is a practical virtue and *more a function of character than of intellect.* It has to do with the handling of everyday affairs and human relationships. A wise man has skill in making his thought issue in worthy action. He is able to discern clearly, judge impartially, choose and decide rightly. He is a man with a broad and deep understanding who can distinguish between good and bad, truth and falsehood. He can assess situations, considering them in their every aspect and giving to each its due weight. He offers sage counsel, and we prefer his advice to that of persons who *may know more but whom we trust less.* He has learned and profited from observation, reflection, and experience. Joy and sorrow, hope, dis-appointment, effort, failure, success—they have all taught him profound lessons and bred in him not only moral perception and a sound sense of values but sympathy and compassion. He can enter into the experience of others, their joys and sorrows, for they are well-nigh as real and vivid as his own. As I write, I have one man in mind. In the view of many, Abraham Lincoln was the wisest and most fundamentally sane man who ever took a great part in the affairs of this country. His was a wisdom both of the heart and the head.

That last sentence should be weighed because wisdom and knowledge must be distinguished. We have far more of the latter than of the former, yet it does not necessarily follow that the more we know the wiser we become. In this century we have made tremendous strides in the acquisition of knowledge. There are things we know that Plato and Paul were ignorant of, but that does not make us wiser than they. It would help in this connection to make a study of the Greek Sophists, as it would to distinguish between sophistication and wisdom. Sir Thomas Browne wrote a book in which he maintained that the idea that the earth went round the sun was too foolish to be controverted. We know better, but we ought not for that reason to suppose that we are wiser than Browne. Wisdom does not depend on factual knowledge. The modern intellectual with all he knows about science and politics and current affairs is inclined to be very conscious of intellectual superiority. He has to be reminded that it is not enough to be familiar with facts; it is necessary to perceive their meaning, to be able to handle them and turn them to good use, which is where our generation with its knowledge of the constitution of the physical universe, with its knowledge of the physiological and psychological constitution of human nature, has so calamitously failed.

A wise man knows more than facts. He has sagacity in the affairs of life, a sagacity rooted in moral integrity and spiritual sensitivity. Wisdom is wider and deeper than intellectual know-how. A man may have a brilliant mind but with it the ignorance of the person who knows nothing except what he sees with his eyes and touches with his fingers. On the other hand, there are people with little formal education who are profoundly wise. They are not brilliant and they may be unlettered, but they have insight and understanding. There is a point to ponder in the saying of Savonarola that "a little old woman who kept the faith knew more than Plato or Aristotle." Knowledge has to do with intellectual activity, wisdom with moral and spiritual activity. We are in the predicament that has overwhelmed us in this century because we are proficient in the one and deficient in the other. We have colossal control of nature but little control of ourselves, and still less of the forces that are bedevilling our civilization.

Long ago the question was asked, "Where is wisdom to be found?" In the main there have been two answers. One is the answer of the pre-Christian world, the world of the Greeks in particular, of Socrates, Plato, and Aristotle. It is a do-it-yourself answer and has its modern counterpart in humanism, in one or other of its many expressions. Wisdom, so the argument runs, is a virtue that can be self-cultivated. It can be achieved by observation, reflection, discipline. Socrates is here the pattern saint. A sentence about him in Plato's *Phaedo* is often quoted: "Of all the men of his time whom I have known, he was the wisest and justest and best." Socrates turned from the study of the physical sciences to the study of human nature. He was to be found in the market place, the stadium, the banqueting hall, among artists, politicians, soldiers. He talked to men about their inner interests and activities, about the validity of their beliefs and values. Concerning any individual attitude, any proposed line of action, any social institution the practical test he raised was, "Is it wise or is it stupid?" He urged people to do what he did, to reflect and meditate about themselves and the life around them, to seek until they found understanding and meaning, and so to arrive at wisdom, moral insight, a true sense of what really matters and of what is most worth living for. Insofar as it seeks wisdom, this is the way taken by our generation, the do-it-yourself way.

To the question "Where is wisdom to be found?" there is another and radically different answer. It is provided by the Bible, exemplified in perfection in Christ, and the first thing to say about it is that the center of interest is shifted from man to God. The Bible does not teach that the secret of living well and wisely lies within our reach and that if we will only apply ourselves and discipline ourselves we can lay hold of it and master it. The Bible takes a dim view of our ability, when on our own, to deal wisely with either personal or social relationships. There are repeated warnings in its pages about the illusion of self-sufficiency, about our capacity to solve all our problems, cure all our ills, eliminate all evils from our world, provided we can manage to attain knowledge and wisdom. It offends us to be told that we are in the position of the boy who was persuaded to stand in a bucket and try to lift himself up by the handle, yet the whole history of man's attempts to deal with the moral problem, which is his basic problem, reveals the extent of his inadequacy. F. L. Lucas quotes Chesterfield as saying, "I am very sure that any man of common understanding may, by proper culture, care, attention and labor, make himself whatever he pleases," and asks, "In what world, one wonders, do people live who can imagine such nonsense?"

"Where can wisdom be found?" The Bible asks that question and the answer it provides is that wisdom is divine in origin. God is all-wise and He is the source and the giver of wisdom. We can have it—if we are to direct our personal lives and the life of our nation aright we must have it—but the way to it is first and foremost through our relationship to God. Contact with Him is its spring and its abiding inspiration. He is not only a person to whom we are accountable but a pattern for our lives. The wise man is the godly man who delights in the law of the Lord and who meditates on it day and night. Wisdom is the ability to look at all things—our personal affairs, our attitude to civil rights, our judgments about international issues—in the light of God. "The fear of the Lord"—fear means not funk but awe and reverence which breed piety—"is the beginning of wisdom." The person who enters into an abiding relationship with God—this is what we see supremely in Jesus—gains from it moral insight, acquires a true discrimination of values, understands what is most worth living for. The word of God which came to one of the biblical writers was: "I shall light a candle of understanding in your heart which shall not be put out."

There is a passage in the Book of Kings that tells how God appeared to the youthful Solomon and said, "Ask what I shall give you." This was Solomon's request: "O Lord my God, thou hast made thy servant king in place of David my father. . . . And thy servant is in the midst of thy people whom thou hast chosen, a great people. . . . Give thy servant therefore an understanding mind to govern thy people, that I may discern between good and evil; for who is able to govern this thy great people?" And God's response was: "Because you have asked this, and have not asked for yourself long life or riches or the life of your enemies, but have asked for yourself understanding to discern what is right, behold, I now do according to your word. Behold, I give you a wise and discerning mind. . . . I give you also what you have not asked, both riches and honor."

In Solomon's prayer there is a guideline for our generation. We incline to be secularists at heart. Ours is a do-it-yourself philosophy. Facing duty and responsibility we tend to rely solely on our own intelligence, and such wisdom as we have is the result of our observation, reflection, experience, all of it limited. There is no dearth of brain power in our society, but there is a lamentable lack of moral insight and a desperate confusion of values. There was in the old world also, and when Paul criticizes the vaunted wisdom of that world and insists that it was not wisdom but folly, it was because he had the same vacuum in mind—intellectual brilliance, reliance on it, and with that reliance the illusion of self-sufficiency; but little moral sense, little perception of true values, and *alienation from God,* their source and inspiration. It is not surprising that wisdom ranks first among the cardinal virtues. Wisdom is one of our deepest needs, is one of civilization's deepest needs. But it is one thing to acknowledge that it is and another to believe, in the words of Scripture, that "it is the breath of the Almighty that gives wisdom" and to order one's life and seek to order the life of society accordingly. Call to mind the exhortation of the New Testament: "If any of you falls short in wisdom, he should ask God for it and it will be given him." Then offer the century-old prayer:

O God, by whom the meek are guided in judgment, and light riseth up in darkness for the godly; grant us, in all our doubts and uncertainties, the grace to ask what thou wouldest have us to do; that the Spirit of wisdom may save us from all false choices, and that in thy light we may see light, and in thy straight path may not stumble. For Christ's sake. Amen.

2. Justice

EVERYWHERE in the world there is a passionate demand for justice. The conviction that all men and all races have an inherent right to life, liberty, and the pursuit of happiness has taken hold of the minds of millions. Deprived of what is their due, multitudes are indignant, are bitter, have risen in revolt feeling that they have nothing to lose but their chains. In our part of the world Communism is commonly regarded as the chief threat to civilization. Is it not rather injustice? Injustice is the fertile soil in which Communism takes root.

What is justice? Noble, high-sounding words do not always lend themselves to simple, straightforward definition. " 'What is truth?' said jesting Pilate and did not wait for an answer." Pilate was familiar with the answers; they were many and varied; he was skeptical of them all. Now, as in his day, there are people who are cynical in their view of justice. One such person defined it as what we decide is in our own interest when we are in positions of privilege and power. The attitude is cynical, but bear in mind the situation back of it and prompting it. The Establishment appeals to law and order; the disestablished to human rights. The propertied class stresses individual liberty and free enterprise; the proletarian class stresses solidarity, trade unions, a controlled society. Both speak of justice, but they do not mean the same thing by it. Often they have no common standards, only those that serve each class in its struggle.

The conviction that has faded in this century is that there is a *divine* standard of justice, eternally valid and applicable to all, regardless of class or race. In its place are human standards, individualistic standards. They are subject to change because they are man-made, and they are shot through with self-interest because there is in man a well-nigh incurable tendency to put himself, his rights, his social group, his country first. The majority of people throughout the world no longer believe in an eternal order of justice which sets a pattern for the life of men and nations.

Communism acknowledges no fixed, immutable principles, no absolute moral order, no divine government of society. But neither does
secularism, which is life lived apart from God and as though He
does not exist, and for the most part the same is true of humanism.
When, as often happens, a contrast is drawn between the religious
West and the godless East, I recall what Sir Walter Moberly wrote
about the modern university in the West: "It neither inculcates nor
expressly repudiates belief in God, it does what is far more deadly,
it ignores Him. In modern universities, as in modern society, some
think God exists, some think not, some think it is impossible to tell,
and the impression grows that it does not matter."[1]

The conception of justice as a cardinal virtue derives from
classical philosophy, Roman as well as Greek, and from Christianity. Plato and Aristotle, Seneca and Marcus Aurelius, thought and
taught constantly about justice. In all of them we note the same
central emphasis: justice consists in giving to everyone what is his
due. Their problem was not with the definition but with its
practical, everyday application. It is no easy matter to determine,
secure, guarantee the specific rights of one man as over against
another, of one class as over against another. On this Aristotle in
particular concentrated, and his analysis of justice has exercised a
profound influence and is reflected in much of the jurisprudence of
the Western world. Common, however, to the greatest of the Greek
and Roman thinkers was the conviction that justice is a cardinal
moral principle because it regulates the relations of men to one
another and is indispensable to—and the foundation of—ordered
society. They went further, for they held that all human law
necessary to the establishment and maintenance of justice is based
on a primal divine law, and that this divine law is the norm, the
standard of all human legislation and jurisdiction.

Christianity absorbed and took over much of this thought and
teaching, but it owed more to the Hebrews than to the Greeks and
Romans. The Old Testament prophets had had a great deal to say
about justice, and what they had to say was in striking contrast to
what came out of Athens and Rome. They were not interested in
ideas or ideals as such; they were not theorists but realists; they
dealt with specifics, not abstractions. Amos, Hosea, Micah, Isaiah,
Jeremiah were passionate advocates of justice and righteousness.
They called for fair dealing between man and man. They made
charges, detailed charges, of glaring injustice, of corruption and
bribery in the courts, of the rich "skinning" the poor. They had a

burning solicitude for the oppressed, the dispossessed, the exploited; for men, women, and children defrauded of their God-given rights. They had little use for the organized religion of their day, and were sure that God had little use for it, because it was silent about social evils, it acquiesced in them, it was itself implicated in them, it bolstered up the status quo. Speaking for God, Amos thundered: "Take away from me the noise of your songs; to the melody of your harps I will not listen. But let justice roll down like waters, and righteousness like an everflowing stream."

Why were they such passionate advocates of justice? For two reasons. First, because of what they believed about God. They were never in any doubt of the standard to which appeal could, should, must be made. It was not a standard they had devised themselves, grasped with their minds; it was not a standard that had evolved in the course of history, a matter of mores and conventions; it was a standard given to them, revealed to them. No less than the Greeks and the Romans they would have said that justice is that which conforms to the norm, but for them the norm was God. God is just. In Him all justice is grounded and from Him it has come forth to men. He deals fairly with men and they are to deal fairly with one another. For the prophets the world with its tangle of justice and injustice was not all there was, and they appealed from it not to an abstraction, an ideal of absolute justice, but to the living God. They affirmed what Abraham before them had affirmed, "Shall not the Judge of all the earth do right?"

The prophets were passionate advocates of justice, first, because of what they believed about God, and second, because of what they believed about man. They held that every man has native, inalienable rights, has an inherent, inviolable dignity, and that both derive from the fact that a personal God creates in His own image and likeness the soul of every individual in the human family. This goes far beyond maintaining that each man is to have his due and if he has it the ends of justice are served. Everything depends on what a man's due is reckoned to be. There are commercial conceptions of justice—what a man's due is in terms of money, wages, a decent livelihood. There are retributive conceptions of justice—what a man's due is in terms of reward for meritorious action or punishment for wrongdoing. Neither of these gets at the fundamental question: What is due a human being simply as a human being, old or young, rich or poor, Jew or Gentile? The answer of the prophets is loud and clear. We all have equal rights, we ought all to be treated alike because we are all the children of one Father. The creation of *all* men in the image of God is the foundation of the sense of justice and the demand for it in the Bible.

In the *whole* Bible, the New Testament as well as the Old. Jesus' teaching about the Fatherhood of God implies and involves not only the brotherhood of man but the rights of man. There are people who say that they do not find any social emphasis in the Gospels, that the religion of Jesus was personal, not social. No social emphasis in the Gospels? Take racism, segregation, discrimination, prejudice. For our Lord they were intolerable, an affront to human dignity. He faced and combatted them all through His ministry. The case is worked out with specifics by Dr. Fosdick. "His people discriminated against the Samaritans. So he told a parable in which a good Samaritan was a hero. They hated the Romans. But he found a Roman of outstanding character and said, 'Truly, I say to you, not even in Israel have I found such faith.' They despised their neighbors, the Sidonians. So he stood up in the pulpit and said. 'There were many widows in Israel in the days of Elijah . . . and Elijah was sent to none of them but only to Zarephath, in the land of Sidon, to a woman who was a widow.' Jesus' central orthodoxy was love for all sorts of people, especially for those against whom other people had a prejudice."[2] And the disciples of Jesus, once they had His mind and shared His spirit, became passionate advocates of human, universal rights. For them all barriers of class and race were down. "God has shown me," said Peter, "that I should not call any man common or unclean." Paul wrote to the Galatians, "There is neither Jew nor Greek; there is neither slave nor freeman; there is neither male nor female. For you are all one in Christ Jesus." When our Lord spoke of how He would judge those who had fed the hungry, given drink to the thirsty, visited the sick and those in prison, He gave an entirely new sanction to the charter of human rights: "As long as you did it for one of these, the least of my brethren, you did it for me."

Some time ago Bishop Pike was taken to task by a group of Episcopal clergymen in Georgia for stating that he did not believe in the Virgin Birth. They charged him with heresy and wanted him disciplined. He made a countercharge. He insisted that the segregation of Negroes and whites in the Episcopal churches of the South is a "heresy really worth discussing." This, quite literally, is what racism is, a heresy—that is, a belief issuing in a practice contrary to the true doctrine of the Church of Christ. There are Christians who

denounce theological heresy to whom it apparently has never
occurred that there is such a thing as ethical heresy; this despite the
warning of Christ, "Not everyone who says to me, 'Lord, Lord,'
shall enter the kingdom of heaven, but he who does the will of my
Father who is in heaven."

God has endowed all men with rights that may not be violated
and that must be respected. This is everywhere the teaching of the
Bible, and all the major church bodies affirm it *in principle*. In
principle; but do we put it into practice? What about our second-
class citizens, our ghettoes, our slums? What about *The Other
America* described by Michael Harrington, the millions of poverty-
stricken citizens in our affluent society? "I tremble for my country,"
Thomas Jefferson said, "when I reflect that God is just." And what
about the poverty, hunger, deprivation, the wretchedness and misery
of millions in Latin America, Africa, Asia? Not to have an
awakened conscience, not to be sensitive to social evils, not to take
any part in righting them, not to be active in promoting and
establishing justice—that is heresy. Christianity is a life before it is
a creed. Of what use is a creed without conduct to match and
validate it?

One thing is stark in its clarity. These are not times for churches
to concentrate only on a narrowly personal religion, on the salvation of the individual but not of society. In the struggle for justice,
for human rights, they must not stand on the sidelines as though
they had no responsibility in such matters. Human relationships are
their responsibility, the more so wherever they are organized in flat
contravention of the mind and spirit and practice of Christ. It is the
business of the churches to lay emphasis on social justice and to
urge and work for the adoption of civil laws which will promote
and maintain it. Samuel Johnson was wide of the mark when he
wrote,

> How small of all that human hearts endure
> That part which laws or kings can make or cure.

To be sure, men cannot be made moral by state and federal
statutes, but this does not exempt churches from responsibility for
just legislation. "Morality," writes Martin Luther King, "cannot be
legislated, but behavior can be legislated. Judicial decrees may not
change the heart, but they can restrain the heartless. The law
cannot make an employer love an employee, but it can prevent him
from refusing to hire me because of the color of my skin. The

habits, if not the hearts, of people have been and are being altered every day by legislative acts, judicial decisions, and executive orders."[3]

There is a broader role today for churches and for Christians. A revolution has been taking place in the way of life of both. Some Christians have gone on a peace march or a freedom ride. Some have taken a stand in their community against segregation in housing. Some on principle and by deliberate choice are residing in integrated dwellings. Some have joined churches committed to integration or are seeking to commit the churches of which they are trustees to integration. Some have introduced fairer practices in hiring labor and job promotion in their place of business. Some have become vocal and active in their support of federal civil rights legislation. As yet they are a minority. The majority of Christians are described in the parody of W. P. Merrill's hymn:

> Stand pat, O men of God.
> The world with problems great
> Has tasks unequal to your strength.
> Stand pat—and make them wait.

What about you? Where do you stand? How do you relate to the challenging problems of society? Is your religion individualistic, monkish? Do you go with it into the thick of the world, or, where your Christianity is concerned, are you like a man who has taken himself out of circulation and gone to live on some small, remote island? There are churches like islands in the sea of life, and Christians who are expatriates. The question each of us ought to face is this: Can I walk humbly with God except as I do justly and love mercy? As to that, the answer of Christ is clear and searching: "Not every one who says to me 'Lord, Lord,' shall enter the kingdom of heaven, but he who does the will of my Father who is in heaven."

NOTES

[1] Sir Walter Moberly, *The Crisis in the University* (London: SCM Press, 1949), p. 55.

[2] Harry Emerson Fosdick, *Dear Mr. Brown* (New York: Harper & Row, 1961), p. 176.

[3] Martin Luther King, Jr., *Strength To Love* (New York: Harper & Row, 1963), pp. 22–23.

3. Temperance

IN church circles the word temperance tends to be given a narrowly restricted meaning. It is applied either to moderation in the use of intoxicating liquors or, and this is the commoner practice, to total abstinence. In the opening years of this century most church temperance societies advocated not moderation but prohibition. There is a story about a priest in Ireland who took temperance for the subject of his sermon and in the course of it declared: "It's whiskey that's the bane of this congregation. It's whiskey that steals away a man's brains. It's whiskey that makes you shoot at landlords and miss them."

The thinkers of the old world, when they made a cardinal virtue of temperance, had more in mind than taking a pledge never to touch strong drink. By temperance they meant power over oneself, control of all one's instincts and passions, mastery of every kind of indulgence. Temperance in that sense was already a traditional virtue in the time of Plato, but he elevated it to the rank of a cardinal virtue, and what he had to say about it had a marked influence not only on subsequent Greek thought, notably the thought of Aristotle, but on Christian thought.

Plato taught that self-discipline with a view to obtaining self-mastery is our first duty. He said that until a man is "master in the house of his own being" he cannot be certain of performing any other duties. He held that a man who cannot master himself is not worthy to rule, and he would have denied such a man—it is a thought to ponder when casting a vote—the right to hold public office. From what one reads and hears about all centers of government there would be a thinning of the ranks of candidates for public office if that rule were enforced. Plato likened the soul to a chariot drawn by two horses, one good and one bad, with a charioteer, reason, directing it. By the good horse he meant the spiritual part of us, and by the bad horse he meant the sensual. They pull in opposite directions, but if there is to be harmony and headway they have to be brought under rational control. Only when they are under such control is it well with the soul.

What Plato had to say about temperance reminds one in some ways of Paul. He had a battle on his hands. He felt the need in his personal life of harmony and integrity. He was aware of forces within him pulling in opposite directions. There was an upward pull and a downward pull, and while his reason responded to the one his will gave in to the other. He told the Corinthians how he disciplined himself to secure self-mastery. "Every athlete," he wrote, "goes into strict training. [Was he thinking of the Olympic games? Had he attended any of them?] They do it to win a fading wreath; we, a wreath that never fades. For my part, I run with a clear goal before me; I am like a boxer who does not beat the air; I pommel my body and make it know its master, for fear [it is a clause that sends a chill through a preacher] that after preaching to others I should be disqualified myself." Think of a man, preaching for a lifetime, being told at the last, "Depart from me, I never knew you"!

There are resemblances between Paul and Plato; there are also differences. For self-control Plato relied on reason, intelligence, good sense. He relied on what the mind can do to move the will, and on what the will can do to avoid excess, control indulgence, regulate instincts and appetites. Paul also relied on his reason and will, put them to work, worked them hard, but they failed him. Like Ovid, he saw and approved the better course, but he followed the worse. With his mind he wanted to do what he knew he ought to do, but he lacked the will power not only to do it but to keep from doing what he knew to be wrong. He got what he lacked from Christ. "Strengthened with might by his spirit in the inner man"—those words bring out the contrast between Paul and Plato, between Christian thought and Greek thought. Faith in Christ is the source and inspiration of mastery over the self. It lays hold of divine power which makes possible what would otherwise be impossible. Reason and will are energized by the indwelling of the Holy Spirit. "Strengthened with might *by his spirit* in the inner man," "the harvest *of the spirit* is . . . self-control"—there is the way to spiritual mastery.

There is another difference between Paul and Plato, between Christian thought and Greek thought. Temperance for the Greeks meant the checking and regulating of animal passions in human nature that were believed to be base. They taught that evil resided in the physical constitution of man. Temperance for Christians is a virtue, a cardinal virtue, not because our physical appetites and instincts are evil and have to be crushed, but because though good and legitimate they have to be brought into the service of the mind and the spirit. There is a phrase in Greek literature—later Greek literature—"the body is a tomb." That is not what the New Testament says. On the contrary, the New Testament teaches that the body is a temple, a temple of God. Christians honor the body as the creation of God, as the agent and instrument of the spirit, as its means of true expression, as the vehicle of man's faculties, of mind, feeling, and will. Christians believe in the incarnation of the Son of God. The New Testament takes high ground. "Glorify God in your body," it says. And again, "Present your bodies a living sacrifice, holy, acceptable unto God, which is your reasonable service." We ought not to think of the body, or of its instincts and appetites, as evil. Every instinct, every appetite of the body is right and good in its own place, and so in its own place is the gratification of every instinct and appetite. It is their intemperate, excessive, perverted use that is evil. What is evil is not their use but their abuse.

Though this is what Christianity teaches, it had to contend from the beginning and has to contend today against the view that the body is evil and that the pleasures of the body, eating, drinking, sex, are reprehensible in themselves. Jesus was no grim ascetic—He came eating and drinking—but a grim asceticism has been practiced by many who call themselves His followers. Some have loathed their bodies, have starved them, or tortured them, or emaciated them by fasting. If Catholic saints have been noted for such austerities, Protestant divines have been noted for their distrust of pleasure as pleasure. They tabooed card-playing and theater-going. They had strict scruples about keeping Sunday—no novel-reading, no swimming, no knitting. They accentuated the negative with a vengeance, put an overwhelming emphasis on "Thou shalt not. . . ." In nineteenth-century Scotland a young minister was brought before the presbytery because on a snowy, icy Sabbath he had skated from one appointment to another. An elderly presbyter fixed on him a forbidding eye and demanded, "Tell me, young man, did ye *enjoy* the skating?"

It is not for asceticism that the New Testament calls but for temperance, the disciplined regulation and control of our appetites and instincts. They are God-given and good in themselves, but their very strength makes it imperative that they should not be allowed to take the upper hand. We have to put curbs and restraints on them. What self-discipline do we impose on ourselves in the matter of sex, eating, drinking, television viewing, the money we spend on ourselves? It is not that these things are evil in themselves, but overindulgence and abuse are evil. William James advised everyone to do something every day for no other reason than that he would rather not do it. It might be added that we should refrain from doing something, if not every day at any rate at frequent intervals, for the very reason that we are prone to pander to ourselves, to our wants and desires, and so much of what we do takes the form of indulgence. The practice of self-mastery even in little things ought not to be made light of. Until we have tried to do it, we do not realize the humiliating fact that we cannot always trust our wills to control our actions. With most of us the body, with its appetites and instincts, is the master and not, as it ought to be, the servant of our spirit. The flesh suffocates the spirit; the spirit is neglected, the flesh pampered. The process can be seen going on every day—men and women becoming heavy, stolid, gross, their appetites uncontrolled, their wills flabby. They practice no voluntary spiritual athleticism.

Protestantism, much of it once fiercely puritanical, is nowadays a slack, easygoing, comfortable religion. If I were asked to single out its greatest weakness, I would incline to say it is unwillingness to practice any sort of stringent religious regimen. Our churches are full of kindly and well-meaning folk, many of them anxious to do good and quick in their appreciation of everything high and lovely, but lamentably lax when it comes to the disciplined practice of religion, regular church attendance, systematic study of the Bible, the saying of their prayers night and morning, or when it comes to the bringing of the body into the service of the soul. The Jew practices self-discipline in observing dietary laws and keeping the Sabbath. The devout Roman Catholic practices self-discipline in going to confession, to early Mass, and in keeping the Church's fast days. The Mormon practices self-discipline in refraining from alcohol, coffee, tea, tobacco, and in giving two years of his life to missionary labor. The Adventist practices self-discipline in keeping Saturday, not Sunday, as the day of rest and in giving scrupulously one-tenth of his net income to the propagation of the Gospel. How do *we* practice self-discipline? In what direction do we practice it? When we detect overindulgence in ourselves, in eating, drinking, smoking, spending—overindulgence as it affects the disposition—

intemperate speech, overweening pride, chronic grumbling—do we take ourselves in hand? Do we ask God for grace and strength to rule ourselves? Which is senior partner in our life—the body or the spirit? The danger for Protestants is that freedom from external observances—fasting in Lent, frequent confession, private penance —may lead to the absence of any disciplined self-control, inner or outer, diet or disposition. Conduct and behavior may not be materially affected at all. There may be no compulsion on the spirit at all. A far cry that from the challenge of Jesus, "If anyone wishes to be a follower of mine, he must deny himself and take up his cross and come with me."

Take the case of smoking. In Lent preachers frequently speak about it. Mostly what they say is that we should discipline ourselves in the matter of smoking, not because it is wrong in itself but because overindulgence is wrong. If the habit threatens to master us we owe it to ourselves to take it in hand. When a man says that he is not going to give up smoking because, when he tries to give it up, he is so ill-tempered that there is no living with him, he is at the place where he ought to take himself in hand. When people say that it is too late for them to stop and that they just don't want to, they have become habit-ridden. Habits should be our servants, not our masters. The person who becomes merely a creature of habit is a poor creature. He ought to keep a stricter rein on himself. "All things," Paul wrote, "are lawful for me, but all things are not expedient; all things are lawful for me: but I will not be brought under the power of any."

That is what the churches have been accustomed to stress in the past. I don't see how they can say *only that* any more. There is no longer any doubt that cigarette smoking is harmful and injurious. It contributes substantially to the death rate. It can cause cancer of the lungs. The Surgeon General's Report of January 22, 1964, found cigarette smoking "the most important cause" of chronic bronchitis. As for coronary artery disease, the leading cause of death in this country, it found that mortality is 70 per cent higher for cigarette smokers than for nonsmokers.[1] The issue, therefore, is no longer moderation in the use of something that affords pleasure. It is a duty to abstain from what is harmful and injurious, and not to abstain is wrong; it is a wrong done to the body. For a long time we have regarded those who would forbid smoking and enforce the veto on everybody as fanatics, or if not fanatics as faddists. There is a new factor to be taken into account now. It is not simply that an intelligent person will ask himself whether a habit should be continued when it is demonstrated that it is injurious and harmful; where physical well-being is involved there is a moral implication involved. Certainly for the Christian, harm done the body is a wrong done the body.

The question of personal example is involved. A father, familiar with the findings of medical science, will not want his son or daughter to become addicted to cigarette smoking. Should he smoke cigarettes himself? In many preparatory schools pupils are forbidden to smoke, and masters are now engaged in heart-searching about their own smoking habits. In 1962 the Royal College of Physicians in Britain issued a report similar in its findings to that of the Surgeon General. Addressing members of the medical profession it stated: "The doctor who smokes cigarettes must, like any other individual, balance the risks against the pleasure he derives from smoking and make his choice. But the doctor who smokes will lessen the effect of public education concerning the consequences of the habit and will find it harder to help his patients who need to stop smoking."[2] The situation is one that calls for personal decision. As citizens we also have a part to play in safeguarding the health of the nation. Public health is a private as well as a public responsibility.

There are wider considerations. Three major broadcasting networks said they would review their policies on tobacco advertising in the light of recent medical findings. They will have to be prompted and prodded or their study may last as long and be as inconclusive as that of the Tobacco Institute. The newspapers of the country should review their policies on tobacco advertising, even though like state and federal officials their publishers are fearful of a heavy loss of income derived from the tobacco industry. To what lengths people will go to make money! It is high time for us to do what Denmark and the Soviet Union are doing—use posters and other publicity means to conduct an educational campaign about smoking. There is a role for the churches, an educational role. They ought not to be silent from any fear of being thought faddist or puritanical. This is not a minor issue but a national one and there is need for public legislation and Christian education.

From the public issue return to the personal one, the broadly personal one, to temperance as disciplined control of one's life and all its appetites and instincts. Remember that while you can use your reason and will in achieving such control, you can rely on a power greater still. "Strengthened with might by his spirit in the inner man!" Faith in Christ is the source and inspiration of temperance. The reason and will are energized by His Spirit dwelling in us. The secret of self-control is Christ-control.

NOTES

1 Dr. Luther L. Terry, *Surgeon General's Report* of January 22, 1964. *New York Times,* January 23, 1964.

2 Quoted in *Our Human Body, Its Wonders and Its Care.* A Library of Fact and Guidance (Pleasantville, N.Y.: The Reader's Digest Association, 1962), p. 154.

4. Courage

COURAGE has been among the most admired of all the virtues. James Barrie said about it: "Courage is the thing . . . the lovely virtue. All goes if courage goes." And he went on to quote Samuel Johnson, "Unless a man has that virtue, he has no security for preserving any other." The generalization, if sweeping, is borne out in everyday experience. Where courage is lacking there is no certain guarantee of integrity. Without it the chances are that the person under pressure will lie when, regardless of the cost, he should speak the truth; he will dissemble when, come what may, he should be the soul of honor; he will give in when he should hold out.

To face a situation from which one inclines to run away, to take hard knocks and come up smiling, to accept a crushing handicap and instead of railing at it as an injustice, turn it from a liability into an asset—who does not applaud such gallantry? The woman, for example, who when troubles came, as they have a habit of coming, not singly but in battalions, remarked to a friend: "I am like a deeply built ship; I drive best under a stormy wind." Or R. L. Stevenson, through years of ill-health refusing, as he put it, to let the medicine bottles on his mantelpiece be the limit of his horizon, and praying: "Give us courage and gaiety and the quiet mind. Give us the strength to encounter that which is to come, that we be brave in peril, constant in tribulation, temperate in wrath, and in all changes of fortune and down to the gates of death, loyal and loving to one another."[1]

I write as one who for almost forty years and at close quarters has watched men and women fighting hard battles. The intrepid fashion in which many of them have stood up to adversity is impressive and humbling. About little things they may have fretted and fumed; about the big crises they were not cowards. They have shouldered heavy burdens with never a word of complaint. They have encountered bravely and without self-commiseration a business reverse, a crippling illness, long, drawn-out anxiety for a loved one. A surgeon, asked how in his experience people faced suffering and death, replied after a moment's reflection that most of them acted like heroes. When the news broke about Captain Scott's death in the Antarctic a journalist wrote: "What splendid people humans are! If there be no loving God to watch us, it's a pity for His sake as much as for our own."

The ancients esteemed courage so highly that they classed it among the cardinal virtues. Their annals are full of tales of men of mighty valor. They lauded physical prowess, the soldier who braved any danger and heroically laid down his life for his country. But they looked on it as a gift of nature and regarded a race like the Spartans as born to know no bodily fear. Endowed with an iron constitution and a strong nerve, a Spartan performed daring exploits in hot blood and with a sudden rush of spirit that a man of frail physique shrank from undertaking. Much as the ancients admired physical courage, however, they recognized moral courage as nobler and rarer. Their highest praise was reserved for men of the stamp of Anaxarchus, who, when ill fortune struck at him blow after blow, declared: "Beat on at the body of Anaxarchus; Anaxarchus himself you cannot touch." For Plato, Socrates was the true hero, playing no tricks with his mind, scorning to compromise with principle, fearlessly championing what was true and just, no matter what the consequence for himself. For the same reason Epictetus the Stoic was held up as a model to emulate. He was a slave in the court of Nero. Anything could happen to anybody in everyday association with a scoundrel like Nero. Did Epictetus live in fear of him? No! "Does the tyrant say he will throw me in prison? He cannot imprison my spirit. Does he say that he will put me to death? He can only cut off my head."

In the literature of Greece and Rome repeated emphasis was placed on the cultivation of courage, the development of inward resources of fortitude which no outward circumstances, however adverse, could exhaust. The young were exhorted to discipline themselves so that when misfortune came their way they would be able to master it—not only endure it without flinching but make a creative use of it and be the better for it. Those beset by calamity were urged not to whimper nor indulge in self-pity but to be strong and play the man. It was the characteristic soul attitude of the Stoic and it has always commanded respect. But there is no gospel in it, no indication of resources of strength beyond the self, nothing but a challenge to self-reliance. When Stoicism has bidden us defy "the slings and arrows of outrageous fortune" and school ourselves to be undaunted by and superior to them, it has no more to say.

In the New Testament little stress is put on the cultivation of courage; the emphasis is of a wholly different kind. A great deal is made of it and for reasons that are obvious enough. To be a Christian nowadays is not generally regarded as an onerous or arduous undertaking. For many it means no more than joining a church, attending it with a fair degree of regularity, contributing to its support. To be a Christian in the first century required courage, physical and moral, of the supreme order. The disciples of Christ were a tiny minority and the servants of a cause that the majority opposed or ridiculed. They were engaged in a battle against heavy odds and ran the risk of persecution, imprisonment, and death. The New Testament employs one figure of strenuous endeavor after another—running, fighting, wrestling, enduring hardship. Paul made frequent use of the military metaphor but his exhortation to the Christian soldier was not to cultivate courage and build up interior resources of stamina; it was to put on the whole armor of God—the helmet of salvation, the breastplate of righteousness, the sword of the Spirit—and be strengthened with might by the same Spirit in the inner man.

The question that arises sooner or later for all of us is where we are to go for courage. Some go no further than themselves. Like the Stoics, they set themselves to develop intestinal fortitude, to discipline themselves to overcome the most formidable of adverse circumstances, to do it without murmuring and complaint, blithely and gaily, "wearing tribulation like a rose." A poet wrote about a woman who drew off life's bitter brew, and by an alchemy she knew, distilled it into laughter. This everybody admires and in days of stress and strain seeks to achieve. Alas, strive as they may, many discover that the springs of endurance in them are too shallow for the incessant demands life makes on them.

Realizing their own inadequacy, some turn for courage to others stronger than themselves. It is a sound instinct. The best and surest way to acquire the lovely virtue is to associate with those who have it. There are more good infections in life than bad ones and courage is unfailingly infectious. The presence of one brave man has always and everywhere been a source of strength and inspiration to his companions and has prevented them from resorting to panicky measures. H. M. Stanley said that when he went to Africa to search for Livingstone he was the biggest atheist in London, but

that when he found him he found God. As day by day in the heart
of the jungle he stood beside Livingstone and saw the heroism of
the man, and how he lived without concern for personal safety or
reputation and only for Africa and Africa's emancipation from
slavery and superstition, he became conscious of a change working
in him. "Livingstone," he wrote, "converted me." Stanley came into
touch with a Christian Greatheart and caught the infection of his
gallant spirit.

On occasions innumerable, courage has come to people in precisely that way, not because they tell themselves to be strong and
play the man, but because others infect them with it. They are
fortunate in having friends who do for them something of what
Churchill did for thousands during the Battle of Britain. There are
times when depressed, disheartened, at the end of their tether, they
find themselves in the company of someone whose faith is firm and
whose personality inspires confidence, and before they quite know
what has happened, hidden springs in them are touched, the
horizons of life are widened, and they are ready once again to quit
themselves like men.

Seeking even greater resources of courage some turn to God. They
school themselves to trust implicitly in His love and power and to
believe that He is nearer, kinder, more ready to help than any
earthly friend. Persuaded that He knows all about their struggle
they take Him into their confidence about everything, go to Him as
a child to his father with their problems, fears, and anxieties. They
reach out into the darkness and find a more than human hand.
They get the horizons of the divine about their life by bringing
God into it.

This is where the contrast of attitude between the Christian
and the Stoic is most marked. Just as much as the ancients, Christ
called for courage. He, too, reckoned it a cardinal virtue. As He
sought to help men and women master the art of living, one of His
watchwords was, "Be not afraid." Day after day He bade His
followers be rid of the fear of man and of the troubles and perils
that would confront them. Whatever the hardships and tribula-
tions, they were to hold on bravely and endure to the end. But the
difference between Christ and the ancients is not in what He said
about the nature or value of courage; it is in what He said about its
source. He put the emphasis on courage not as a matter of physical
constitution, or as a moral virtue to be self-sustained, but as the
outcome and consequence of faith in God. He was sure, having

proved it in His own experience, that when men have the confidence that God is with them and supporting them they can meet all the circumstances of life fearlessly and cheerfully.

The assurance has been validated from generation to generation in the experience of the followers of Christ. They have had "courage, gaiety and the quiet mind," not because they had the physique of a Samson or a Hercules but because they drew on divine power. Luther was a man for all seasons. A cardinal legate stormed at him: "Do you expect your princes to take up arms to defend you—a wretched worm like you? I tell you, No! And where will you be then? Tell me that! Where will you be then?" "Then, as now," answered Luther, "in the hands of Almighty God." Lincoln was a man's man, never striking sail to a fear, staunch and unswerving in principle, his heart undaunted and his honor unsullied through years of conflict and crisis; but his fortitude was not self-sustained. "I have been driven many times to my knees," he testified, "by the overwhelming conviction that I had nowhere else to go. My own wisdom and that of those around me seemed insufficient for the day." Dietrich Bonhoeffer was imprisoned in Buchenwald by the Gestapo. One Sunday he was conducting a service for his fellow prisoners and had just pronounced the benediction when the door opened and two officials entered and said, "Prisoner Bonhoeffer, get ready to come with us." For every man in the room those words "come with us" meant one thing only—the scaffold. They bade Bonhoeffer good-by. Drawing one of them aside he said, "This is the end—for me the beginning of life."[2] The next day he was hanged.

Courage is the lovely virtue. We all admire and covet it. Up against difficult situations we call upon ourselves to be plucky, to face the chances and changes of life without whining and with gallantry, never to turn our back but march breast forward. Yet the reserves of endurance in us may not match the demands made on us. Even the finest courage wears thin unless it is fortified by something beyond courage. One of the saddest things in life is to see people sore bestead, taking hard knocks, trying to put a brave face on things, desperately in need of sustenance but not going to the place above any other where sustenance can be found. When I see them, and in my calling scarcely a week passes but I do, John Ruskin's saying comes to my mind: "I am not surprised at what people suffer; I am surprised at what they miss." A man with a fight on his hands exhorts himself: "Don't whine; don't let this get you down; stand up to it and master it." If only that were enough! It is all that some find to say, but it is not all that there is to say. There is a deeper source of courage. Faith in ourselves we need, but we can go on to undergird it with faith in God. We can tell Him what we are up against, can confide in Him and trust Him to help us, can get the horizon of the divine about our life. "No one," the Bible promises, "who puts His trust in Him will ever be disappointed; no one." Spiritual resources are available not only to a few choice souls, a spiritual elite; they are within the reach of all who have the will to draw on them.

Something that Wendell Phillips said at the height of the struggle for the abolition of slavery points up the reason for the valor of every Christian Greatheart. "It is easy to be brave when all behind you agree with you, but the difficulty comes when nine hundred and ninety-nine of your friends think you are wrong. Then it is the brave soul who stands up, one among a thousand, but remembering that one with God makes a majority." If we remember that we shall not lack courage.

NOTES

1 R. L. Stevenson, *Valaima Papers* (New York: Charles Scribner's Sons).

2 Dietrich Bonhoeffer, *Prisoner for God* (New York: The Macmillan Co., 1960), p. 12.

5. Faith

WE have seen that four virtues—wisdom, justice, temperance, courage—were held to be fundamental by ancient moralists in Greece and Rome. They taught that if a man was to attain fitness and fullness of life those were the virtues he must cultivate. They pointed to them as the basic elements of character, the essential principles of conduct, the cornerstones of civic rectitude. To be without them was to have a defective, a maimed character.

All four virtues were taken over by Christianity. However, recognizing that they had reference chiefly to man's life in relation to himself and to society, it added three more—faith, hope, and love. It said these stood for the divine element in man and that they were expressive of his relation to God and the spiritual world. The first four came to be spoken of as natural, the last three as supernatural or theological. In all they make seven, the mystic, perfect number, and over against them Christianity set the seven deadly sins.

It will help our understanding of the meaning of Christian faith if we are clear first of all as to what it is not. It is not *credulity*. In *Through the Looking-Glass* the White Queen claims she is a hundred and one years, five months and one day old. "I can't believe *that!*" says Alice. "Can't you?" answers the Queen. "Try again: draw a long breath and shut your eyes." This is Christian faith as some conceive it—a strain on the intelligence, the blind acceptance of archaic and obsolete beliefs, intellectual suicide. A character in one of Arthur Koestler's books says to a priest: "I won't have any of your patent medicine. What you ask of me is the unconditional surrender of my critical faculties." But that is a misconception. Faith is not credulity. What is the first and great commandment? "Thou shall love the Lord thy God with all thy heart and with all thy soul and with all thy strength and *with all thy mind.*" To think, to think honestly and fearlessly, is a Christian duty. To believe without thinking honestly and fearlessly is superstition. To refuse to profess faith in what one does not believe is not a sin; it is a virtue. If I believe that God is truth I must reject what is untrue. At the same time I am bound to keep in mind that I am a finite being, that there are limits to my understanding, that there is a great deal I do not know. In the sciences it is proverbial that the more profound the scholar, the greater is his humility—Sir Isaac Newton comparing himself to a child gathering a few shells on the shore of an illimitable ocean. It does not occur to the scientist to say that because he does not understand a thing it cannot be so. He appreciates that his intellectual equipment can grasp bits of reality but not the whole of it.

Again Christian faith is not *credence and nothing else*. It is not solely subscription to abstract religious truths. It is more than intellectual assent to what the Bible and the Church teach about God and Christ. Orthodoxy is not faith and is no substitute for faith. Acceptance of a creed, the Apostles' Creed say, and the recital of it in church on Sunday is one thing; belief in a person, in Jesus Christ, is another. This is the fundamental weakness in the case of many. They pay lip service to Christianity. They have inherited their religion as one comes by a family heirloom. They are Christian because their parents and grandparents were Christians. They have never given much serious consideration to what Christian faith is or to what it demands. They have been content to let others do their thinking for them and have taken over at second hand and without scrutiny or inquiry the common run of conventional belief. "A man," wrote John Milton, "may be a heretic in the truth; if he believes things only because his pastor says so, or because the assembly so determines, without knowing other reasons, though his belief be true, yet the very truth he holds becomes his heresy." Such passive acceptance, whether of the teaching of the Bible or of the affirmations of the creeds, or of the basic doctrines bound up with the Christian outlook on life, is not faith.

What is Christian faith? It is more than a form of knowledge; it is a fact of experience. It is more than intellectual assent; it is wholehearted trust. It is reliance placed primarily not on a proposition but on a person. To have faith in God is to have confidence in His presence and power and trustworthiness. It is to enter into an intimate, individual relationship with Him, to have dealings with Him, to become obedient to His commands, to live one's life with Him in control. Hartley Coleridge wrote about it:

Think not the faith by which the just shall live
Is a dead creed, a map correct of heaven,
Far less a feeling fond and fugitive,
A thoughtless gift, withdrawn as soon as given,
It is an affirmation and an act
Which makes eternal truth be present fact.

It is not only an act, it is an attitude, a life attitude, and far from being passive is a powerful and creative moral force. It is a plain fact of everyday life that faith of this dynamic kind, rooted in personal conviction and issuing in personal commitment, can transform character and conduct. To the assertion that faith is an opiate, the eleventh chapter of Hebrews is the best of answers. The writer sees faith as the vital virtue in all the heroes and saints whose names he records. Through faith their weakness was turned into strength. They overthrew kingdoms, established justice, saw God's promises fulfilled. Faith made them what they were and enabled them to do what they did, and because of it they have their names written forever in history and have made it easier for succeeding generations to believe in the unseen world and in God.

Think of Jesus and of what, day after day, He urged on men and women: Believe in the presence and power of the living God. By complete trust in your heavenly Father banish anxiety and care from your lives. Go into your room, shut the door, and pray to Him. "Have faith in God," He said. "Have no fear—only believe." "Anything can be done for anyone who believes." When He found this trustful confidence in God He rejoiced. When He failed to find it He was surprised and troubled. In the presence of stolid unbelief in Nazareth, His home town, His will to heal was paralyzed. "He could do no mighty works there because of their unbelief." And He practiced what He preached. In Him we see faith in action. From first to last He trusted God. He never lost the confidence that Love was at the heart of things. He staked all on the absolute Power of that absolute Love. He went all over Palestine offering one sublime assurance. God is more near, more real, more gracious, more ready to help every one of us than any one of us realizes. He is incomparably better than the very best we can think of Him, far better than we deserve. He is always seeking a deeper intimacy of trust and affection with every human being. He is the source and the inspiration of our sense of right and wrong; and He is on the side of right. He will yet make one family out of this sinful world. In spite of all appearances to the contrary He reigns, and governs as well as reigns.

There is a paragraph in David Cairns' *The Faith That Rebels*, a book not to be unread because published as long ago as 1928, which brings out movingly what faith signified for Jesus and shows its relevance to personal life today.

Turning again to the Gospel narrative, we find Christ's call for faith on one and all around Him so constant that one cannot but feel that if He were here in the body in the world once more, and we all gathered round Him, and each of us told Him in turn the story of our failures and tragedies and sins, He would say to each of us: "What has been wrong with you, and what is wrong with you still, is that as yet you have not enough faith in God. You think that the trouble has been due to your indolence, your hatred, and your pride. It may be, but there is something deeper. You must have faith in God. If you realize that, all evil and tragic things will lose their power.[1]

That is deeply moving. If it is true it is wonderful. But is it true? Not at the top of our minds but at the bottom of our hearts, do we believe it to be true? Do we believe in a God like the God in whom Jesus believed, gracious, loving, powerful, and in sovereign control of the universe? In sovereign control of the universe! It doesn't look like it. Humanity blunders on from crisis to crisis, as it has done in generation after generation. Devilish weapons of destruction are being manufactured that can bring civilization to a sudden and terrible end. We, with all our religious and humanitarian professions, claim to have more of them than Russia. There is goodness in the world but the evil in it is persistent and aggressive. Is it chronic, endemic, inveterate as well? Christians go to church and sing,

> The Lord is King! lift up thy voice
> O earth, and all ye heavens rejoice;
> From world to world the joy shall ring,
> The Lord Omnipotent is King!

But when Walter Lippmann wrote *Preface to Morals* he set down on the opening page, "Whirl is King, having driven out Zeus."[2] It was a quotation from Aristophanes. Think of Aristophanes making such an affirmation over two thousand years ago, and of Lippmann picking it up and using it as descriptive of the world nineteen hundred years after the advent of Jesus.

We are faced with a haunting question: Was Jesus right or wrong? When we think of the faith from which He never swerved we cannot but ask: Was He deceived, or is He a faithful witness, the herald of the truth of truths? Everything turns on whether in this central matter, faith in a God of love and power, Jesus was a visionary, a dreamer, or, as Carlyle expressed it, "a Son of Fact," His spirit broad awake to the biggest Fact in life, the Clue to the riddle of existence. There are some who cannot believe in Him or in His heavenly Father, though they long to believe in something, and they sense and sometimes say that the only hope for individuals and for the world is the emergence of some new transcendental faith which will re-establish man's relations with the world and give him something to live and die for other than expediency. As for those of us who are Christians, we stake all on the conviction that Jesus is right, that the real forces that rule the world are spiritual, that there is a power at work in it that can surmount evil, that love is at the heart of things and creation's final law, that over and above all is a God of goodness and grace. Our minds are made up. We say what Donald Hankey said on the Flanders battlefield: "Faith is betting your life that there is a God," the God and Father of our Lord Jesus Christ. We resolve to live and work and, when the time comes, to die by what seems to us the noblest hypothesis. Faith for us is confidence in Jesus, commitment to Him, belief in His revelation of God and what flowed from it, His Mind and Spirit, His way of life, His basic principles—the Fatherhood of God and the Brotherhood of Man.

How can a person who does not have this faith get it? How can a person who had it but has lost it regain it? Observe what Jesus said about that. He urged people *to do something* in order to come into possession of faith. To one man He said, "Follow me." He told the rich young ruler to go and sell all he had and give to the poor. When asked the speculative question, "Are there few that be saved?" He replied with the practical exhortation, "Strive to enter in at the strait gate." He said that to have the will to do God's will is the first step on the road to faith. Why did He place such stress on action? Was it not because, though faith involves the mind, it is not primarily an intellectual problem? Believing is fundamentally the giving of ourselves to something in order to discover the truth of it. There are many things that do not reveal their reality to us until we give ourselves to them—appreciation of music, mastery of a language, the experience of love. With faith it is the same. It begins as an experiment and becomes an experience. A student spoke of his religious difficulties to a friend. "But you are living wholly in your negations," the friend said. "Go to your room, take a sheet of paper, and write down all the things which you do believe beyond

question and on which you are willing to act." The advice was
sound. Don't live in your negations. Live in the direction of your
beliefs.

A story related by Thomas à Kempis (was it his own story?) sums
up the whole matter.

There was once a man, anxious in mind, wavering between doubt and
faith; till a time came when he could bear his troubles no longer, and he
threw himself before an altar in a church: and he said to himself again
and again: "If I could only know that I should always remain faithful!"
And all of a sudden he heard an answer in his heart, as if from God: "And
if you did know, what would you do then? Do it now, and your care will
be gone." Comforted and strengthened he at once committed himself to
the divine will. And after that he was no more inquisitive to know what
might happen to him in the future; he tried only to find out what was
the acceptable and perfect will of God, so as to begin every good work
and to continue it.[3]

NOTES

[1] David Cairns, *The Faith That Rebels* (New York: Doubleday, Doran & Co.,
1928), p. 210.

[2] Walter Lippmann, *Preface to Morals* (New York: The Macmillan Co., 1930),
p. 1.

[3] *Imitation of Christ*, Bk. I, Ch. 25.

6. Hope

IN the ancient world outside of Israel little was said about hope. No one in Greece or Rome thought of making hope a cardinal virtue. At best it was an incentive to action, yet it was of doubtful value. As often as not it was a will-o'-the-wisp, elusive, misleading, an illusion; if it helped some to endure life, in the case of others it meant that their spirits were raised only afterward to be dashed. Lord Brougham, a Victorian pagan, inscribed on his villa in Cannes a typical Greek epitaph:

> I've entered port. Fortune and Hope, adieu!
> Make sport of others, for I've done with you.

In the world of our day hope is not the prevailing temper. Franz Mehring, the German historian and socialist, was convinced that at the stroke of midnight on the New Year's Eve that marked the transition from the nineteenth to the twentieth century, a new and glorious era would come into being. There were many at the turn of the century who believed progress was inevitable and had boundless faith in the future of civilization. Then there came a world war, after it a world-wide depression, after it a second world war, after it a cold war, and now nuclear weapons pose a threat to the survival of civilization. Misgivings about the future and gloomy forebodings as to what lies ahead of the human race are everywhere. There is disenchantment with science, government, political programs; former Communists, for example, complaining that Communism started as a movement of liberation and became a tyranny. There is skepticism about the possibility of establishing a better order of society. In 1964 a book was published in Britain with the title, *Suicide of a Nation?*[1] It is a symposium and has seventeen contributors. The general tone of the book is that education is hopeless, Parliament amateurish, industry at a standstill, society conformist. One of the contributors writes: "Sometimes I think the England I know now is like a parent who has had a first stroke." It is not difficult to envisage a book of a similar sort appearing in our country and in other countries. This, to be sure, is only one aspect of the case. There are people in large numbers who are looking and working for a better order of society, "the Great Society," who rely on education and science to promote it, and who are confident that mankind has enough good sense and good will to advance it. Nevertheless hope is not the prevailing temper of the times; pessimism is in the air we breathe.

This, the prevalence of pessimism in the ancient world and in the modern world, makes all the more remarkable what we find when we read the New Testament. Nowhere from beginning to end, nowhere in the record of the original and genuine Christian life, is there a single word of despondency or gloom. It is the most buoyant, exhilarating, and joyful book that was ever written. Hope surges in it. The word and the thing are on page after page. It takes its place with faith and love as one of the three cardinal and distinctive Christian virtues. The men and women we read about in the narrative of the events following the resurrection of Christ do not come together to discuss the meaninglessness of life, the absurdity of existence, their homelessness in a neutral universe. Much of our contemporary literature presents a shatteringly pathetic picture of man. He is "lonely," a "stranger," an "outsider." He lives in a state of "tragic ambiguity." He feels "hollow" and "alienated" and is subject to "anguish" and "despair." The first Christians used some of those very terms, but to describe people round about them who were "without hope and without God in the world." They never spoke about themselves in such terms, never asked, "What is the meaning of life? Is it going somewhere? Has it a purpose and goal?" Christ put into their hands the clue to life's meaning, gave them a world they could live in, a self they could live with, a cause and a Master they could live for and die for. Their faith in Him, the Pioneer of life, the Conqueror of death, the Savior of the world, inspired in them a boundless hope for the future.

The New Testament, it should be emphasized, is a soberly realistic book. It does not shrink from an honest reading of the facts. How could it, telling as it does about the best life that man has ever known put to an open shame and crucified, telling about Caiaphas, Pilate, Judas, the craven disciples, the revengeful mob, all of them having modern counterparts? What it says about human nature is not flattering. It says that we are all without exception sinners. We are liable to take offense when told that. For the most part we associate sin with glaring evils, with crooks, drunkards, sexual perverts, whereas the New Testament sees the root of sin in something that is in all of us, a hard core of self-centeredness, the disposition to put ourselves before either God or our neighbor. It says that with this root of evil in us we cannot live up to our own ideals; that man, whether man the individual or man in society, cannot be what he wants to be or do what he wants to do but is always dogged by self-contradiction, by failure and frustration. It says that man, individually and collectively, is fundamentally incapable of resolving his problems. His dreams, ideals, utopias—a war to end war, the world made safe for democracy, a just and durable order of society—are never fully realized, are often blasted; his pride, egotism, will-to-power block the way to their fulfillment. This is not popular teaching. We dislike and resent it, but can we deny its truth?

We can do amazing things in industry, science, and technology. Telstar is a marvelous achievement, as is the electronic computer that predicts the final result in the early hours of an election night. But some of the greatest of our inventions, if they should be put to use, can only mean wholesale self-destruction. The commercial jet plane is a triumph of engineering, the intercontinental bomber a diabolical device. Nuclear weapons symbolize the fact that our best efforts are powerless to secure for us a harmonious and peaceful world. And this is what has all along been happening. Our situation today is typical of what has always been man's predicament. Take into account the history of civilizations, their rise and fall, the moral rot that sapped and undermined them, the biblical verdict on them—"weighed in the balances and found wanting." Take into account the history of revolutions, how they start with ideals of liberty, equality, and fraternity and turn into their opposites: the French Revolution, then the Napoleonic wars, then the triumph of reaction; the Russian Revolution, the vision of a classless society, then a tyranny brutal and unscrupulous. Take into account the attempt to establish a League of Nations after the first World War and the outbreak in 1938 of a second World War. Take into account how we fought the totalitarianism of the Nazis and Fascists and in doing so became more and more totalitarian ourselves. This is our human predicament; our inability, notwithstanding our repeated and concerted attempts, to resolve our problems. And this is why in the Bible hope is not man-centered but God-centered.

Despite the reality and persistence of sin in individual and collective life the Bible sets no limits to the power of God to make new men and a new society. God, it says, is present and active in history. He has entered into it in Christ to transform human nature and human society. He has revealed in the life, death, and resurrection of Christ the meaning of human existence. History is being guided by a divine mind to a good and beneficent end. It is not a futile cycle of birth and death, a sorrowful wheel endlessly revolving; civilizations like individuals, born only to die and be buried; no future for the world save a tragic repetition of what has already been—great movements, religions, social revolutions springing up, full of high ideals and the most wonderful promise, but the hopes of their founders never fulfilled, the world blundering on in its old unhappy way, muddling along from crisis to crisis. History is the sphere of the creative energies of God. He is controlling its course, inaugurating new eras, raising up leaders, directing the destiny of nations. It is not a never-ending repetitive process but—to quote Toynbee—the masterful and progressive execution of a divine purpose which is revealed to us in fragmentary glimpses and transcends our human powers of vision and understanding in every dimension.[2] This is the theme of one of our best-loved hymns, with the refrain: "Our God is marching on." The goal of history is the Kingdom of God. The agelong warfare between good and evil will not drag on and on indefinitely and inconclusively. One day it will end, and end in the victory of righteousness and God. This is the living hope inspired by Christ. This is the faith of the Christian. To the unbelief which says that history is a dingdong battle all the way between good and evil with nothing in it to prove that the good will ever finally overcome the evil, Christian faith replies with the tremendous affirmation, "The kingdoms of this world are become the kingdom of our Lord, and of his Christ; and he shall reign for ever and ever."

This is our historic faith. Millions cannot share it. To multitudes it is the hardest part of the Christian creed. They see no pattern in history, no master plan, no increasing purpose running through the ages. The plight of the world and of humanity is such that it seems to them simpler to conclude that "Whirl is King" than that the Lord is King. What guarantee have you, they ask us, that in the long run what you call God's purposes will prevail? At best are you not resting everything on a belief for which there is no rational, empirical demonstration? We have to acknowledge that we can offer no demonstrable proof. Ours is a judgment of faith, maintained against heavy odds and in the face of much that makes it look false and foolish. It is not an inference drawn from a survey of history but an intuitive certitude which no contemplation of the darkness and mystery of life can shake. Something deeper than intellect is involved. We say with the writer of the Epistle to the Hebrews, "Faith gives substance to our hopes, and makes us certain of realities we do not see." It is Christ who inspires our faith. In His life and death and resurrection we see as it were in miniature, the world struggle and the final issue of it. The dark night of Calvary was followed by the dawn of Easter Day. The resurrection is our assurance of the ultimate triumph of goodness and God. It illustrates the way in which God is present and active in history. He did not interfere at Calvary to save the innocent Sufferer. Human malice and passion were permitted to do their worst. Having given man a free will God did not take it away. Yet He brought good out of evil and victory out of defeat. So it was then. So we believe it will be at the consummation of all things. Righteousness will be vindicated; justice will be done; God will be all in all.

We do not know when the consummation of all things will take place, when the Kingdom of God will be fully and finally established. There are Christians who believe that the world will grow worse and worse and that the only hope for it is the end of it. There are Christians who believe that the world will grow better and better and that their mission is to "bring in the day of brotherhood and end the night of wrong." There are Christians who believe that the Kingdom of God will come fully and finally not on earth but in heaven, not in time but eternity; that history has a meaning, but a meaning beyond itself; that this world is intelligible only in relation to another world. *What do you believe?* Oblige yourself to face the issue fairly and squarely. It is a historian, Herbert Butterfield, who writes: "Our final interpretation of history is the most sovereign decision we can take, and it is clear that every one of us has to take it for himself. It is our decision about religion, about our total attitude to things, and about the way we will appropriate life. And it is inseparable from our decision about the role we are going to play ourselves in that very drama of history."[3] Even so, the fact is that we do not know when the Kingdom will come, or in what manner, or by what stages. We do well to remember the words of Jesus: "About that day or that hour no one knows, not even the angels in heaven, not even the Son; only the Father." And again: "It is not for you to know about dates or times which the Father has set within his own control." Those words, addressed to the first

Christians, apply to us. We do not have knowledge of the long-term strategy of God but we are assured, Christ has assured us, of the ultimate victory of God.

And we know where our task lies. We cannot "bring in" the Kingdom but we are the servants of the King and dedicated to the furtherance of the Kingdom here and now. This is what gives meaning, mission, destiny to our lives. Think of the apostles with that for their conviction—servants of the King and of the Kingdom —setting on foot the conversion of the Roman Empire. Think of Wilberforce with that for his conviction, toiling for the abolition of slavery; of Carey going to India and Trevor Huddleston to Africa and Tom Dooley to Asia. A revived belief in God and in the Kingdom of God and in our call to be servants of the Kingdom would be an unending stimulus and would work wonders in the Church and the world. At an international missionary conference William Temple stated the case thus: "This is the constancy that the Gospel gives us. Our starting point is fixed: it is the creative love of God. Our goal is fixed: it is the realized Kingdom of God. And our way to the goal is fixed: it is found in Him who said, 'I am the Way.' "[4]

NOTES

[1] A. Koestler, ed., *Suicide of a Nation?* (London: Macmillan & Co., 1964).

[2] Arnold J. Toynbee, *Civilization on Trial* (New York: Oxford University Press, 1948), p. 14.

[3] Herbert Butterfield, *Christianity and History* (New York: Charles Scribner's Sons, 1950), p. 25.

[4] William Temple, *Christian Faith and Life* (New York: The Macmillan Co., 1931), p. 28.

7. Love

LOVE as the word is used in the New Testament was practically unknown in the ancient world. It is not too much to say that it was a new virtue. It has been called the discovery of Christianity, and from the first this was its master-word, its inner secret and outward sign, its distinctive and unique characteristic. If we are asked to sum up in a single word what Christianity is, the answer is love. "If I have no love," Paul wrote, "I am nothing." Here is the bedrock of Christian character, not simply one virtue among many but the virtue from which all the others have their rise. Every excellence of character springs from it and exhibits it. Love begets wisdom, tempers justice, instills courage, inspires temperance, is the source of faith and hope.

The word is in constant use, yet there is scarcely another in our language conveying so many sorts and shades of meaning. In connotation it ranges all the way from lust and lechery to the sublimest sacrificial devotion. We can only judge its meaning from its context, as a few examples will show. "The love of money is the root of all evil." "In love of home, the love of country has its rise." "The word liberty in the mouth of Mr. Webster sounds like the word love in the mouth of a courtesan." "The love of Christ constrains us." These are common usages, and in each instance the word means something different. Acquisitive greed, family affection, patriotism, lust, devotion to Christ, are all indicated by the employment of the same term. Aldous Huxley complained that love is greasy from being fingered by Stigginses. There ought, he felt, to be some way of dry-cleaning and disinfecting words. He compared words like love, purity, goodness, and spirit to a pile of dirty linen waiting for the laundress.

It is a handicap that the English language has only one word for love and that it has to express such varied meanings. The Greek language in which the New Testament was written has several: *eros*, which in the main denotes sexual passion; *epithumia*, which denotes desire, particularly with reference to forbidden things, and which is sometimes translated "lust"; *philia,* familiar to us in philanthropy, good will to all mankind. The New Testament brings into special prominence a fourth word, *agape,* remints it, charges it with fresh meaning, puts it at the center of everything that has to do with the relation of God to man and of man to his brother man.

Agape, Christian love, denotes a great deal more than personal liking and warmth of affection. It involves volition as well as emotion. It stands for active good will shown to all, going beyond the boundaries of family, class, nation, and including enemies, given without limits or conditions, not only to the attractive and deserving but to the unattractive and the undeserving. Said Aristotle, "Only what is worthy to be loved can be an object of friendship." Christianity cuts diametrically across that position. Love, it says, asks no questions about the nature or worth of the person to be loved; it loves unconditionally, without regard to merit or desert, loves the unlovely, the unloving, the unloved.

This is what God does. He has no ill will toward anybody. He makes the sun rise on good and bad alike, and sends the rain on the honest and the dishonest. He loves us every one as though there were but one of us to love. He loves freely, spontaneously, above and beyond all our deserving. This is what God *does* because this is what He *is.* He loves us because He is love, because love is the essence of His inmost personal being. As one of the profoundest passages in the New Testament puts it, "Beloved, let us love one another, for love is of God, and every one who loves is born of God and knows God; he who does not love, does not know God, for God is love."

For Christ the supreme principle is the love principle. Consider His teaching about the love of God; for example, the Parable of the Prodigal Son. It is told to make one fact crystal clear. God is our Father, and though we turn from Him, forget Him, fall far below His plan for us, He never ceases to love us, is always willing to forgive our waywardness, is always eager and ready to make an end of our self-willed estrangement and alienation and welcome us home. Consider Christ's teaching about the love we are to have for our fellows, taking in illustration another parable, that of the Good Samaritan. The story tells of an active good will that surmounts all barriers, whether of religion or race. There are no limits to its outreach; it is not hedged about by restrictions of class or caste, worth or merit. Let it see human need of any kind at any time or anywhere, and at once it goes into action. For such active good will "caring is the greatest thing; caring matters most."

Christ reveals what love is even more by His life and death than by His teaching. He spent Himself, "emptied" Himself, literally gave Himself away, unreservedly and unconditionally. He went where the clergy of His day would never have thought of going, went where need called regardless of reputation, sat often at outcasts' tables, never gave anybody up in disgust or reckoned anybody as beyond redemption, earned the name "friend of publicans and sinners." Day after day He devoted Himself to the service of the sick and the sinful, and when He died it was on a cross, in agony of body and soul. Yet even in His agony and despite the betrayal of Judas, the desertion of His disciples, the hatred of the ecclesiastics, the brutality of the soldiers, the apathy of the public, He prayed, "Father, forgive them, for they know not what they do." Afterward, His followers saw the same motivation in His death as in His life. He died as He lived, with love in His heart. For Him there was one great absolute: overcome evil with good and hate with love.

It is to this that Christians are committed—that God is love, that man is made for love, that all the world over, the human heart is the same, and love is the way to it. "Name one harlot," someone has said, "who has ever been reclaimed by treating her as a harlot." And we may add: Name one enemy who has ever been reclaimed by treating him as an enemy. Those who dismiss this as too idealistic for the relations of men and nations ought to think more deeply about the direction in which the world is moving. When they say that love won't work in a fiercely competitive society, they should face the question whether the admittedly unidealistic and supposedly practical principle of the survival of the strongest is working. We are seeking to bolster up our way of life by crude force, yet what is happening is that not merely our way of life but the survival of the race is in jeopardy. Out of the thunder of contemporary events one fact is emerging: the obligation of humanity to live by the love principle if it is to live at all. The alternative is—love or perish!

Christians are not solitary voices in sounding that warning. There are *humanists* who are stressing it. Bertrand Russell, author of a book entitled *Why I Am Not a Christian*, surprised an audience by stating: "The root of the matter if we want a stable world is a very simple and old-fashioned thing, a thing so simple that I am almost ashamed to mention it, for fear of the derisive smiles with which wise cynics will greet my words. The thing I mean is love, Christian love. If you feel this, you have a motive for existence, a guide in action, a reason for courage, an imperative necessity for intellectual honesty."[1]

There are *scientists* making the same emphasis. Dr. J. Robert Oppenheimer was invited to deliver a nation-wide broadcast marking the end of Columbia University's yearlong bicentennial celebrations. The press reported that in his address he "set a path for mankind" and "outlined his philosophy for a changing world." The concluding words of the broadcast were: "This cannot be an easy life. We shall have a rugged time of it to keep our minds open and to keep them deep . . . in a great open windy world; but this is, as I see it, the condition of man; and in this condition we can help, because we can love one another."[2] Think of it! The one-time head of the Los Alamos project exhorting world strugglers—in the very words of the New Testament—to "love one another."

Something of the same sort many *novelists* are urging, Carson McCullers, Alan Paton, Richard Ellison, to name three. In their writing love has a special character and urgency and is viewed as the only recourse against frustration, isolation, and a sense of meaninglessness. The one way to define and discover the self, they say, is to get beyond the self through love. Without this, in a time of unstable values and totalitarian ideologies, human impulses become violent, predatory, and destructive. The stress is on communication through communion, and accompanying it a reaction against totally political solutions. What one novelist after another is maintaining is that simple human affection can always be counted upon, and that without love life and life's meaning are lost.

Love or perish! For years this is what *psychologists* have been telling us, Freud and Fromm, Suttie and Menninger. Love is not just a matter of religious idealism. It is the indispensable emotion. Men can no more live without it than they can live without breathing. The twentieth century has brought insights and discoveries in the psychology of love and hate which are in their way as startling as the discoveries of modern physics. It is a strange historical coincidence that during the years when man learned to unchain the destructive forces inherent in matter he also learned more than ever about the nature of destructiveness within himself. He has learned that hate, resentment, hostility, and fear work like poisons, that they actually affect the secretions of the body and induce disease. In an age when man has brought his power of subduing nature to such a pitch that by using them he could exterminate life, he has learned that love is the one essential vitamin of the soul, that his need of it is as great as his need for food and drink, that he sentences himself to alienation and self-destruction when he spurns it, when he hates and fights and will not live in peace and good will with his fellows.

A missionary in Africa whose wife had died on the mission field was furloughed home. Together with his small son he set out, first by wagon over bumpy paths and roads, then by steamer. On the ocean rough weather was encountered, and the boat began to pitch and roll. "Daddy," the boy asked, "when will we have a home that won't shake?" That boy was making a query for the whole human race. And the mounting testimony that comes from humanists, scientists, novelists, psychologists, is that man is sinning against the very nature of things when he lives without love. He is made for it, hungry for it, unhappy and frustrated without it. It is the greatest thing he knows, the stable element in an unstable world, the ultimate meaning of life because it is the groundwork of the universe. A poem called "Ultimatum" sums up the human predicament.

> Now the frontiers are all closed.
> There is no other country we can run away to.
> There is no ocean we can cross over.
> At last we must turn and live with one another.
>
> We cannot escape this day any longer.
> We cannot continue to choose between good and evil
> (The good for ourselves, the evil for our neighbors);
> We must all bear the equal burden.
>
> At last we who have been running away must turn and face it.
> There is no room for hate left in the world we must live in.
> Now we must learn to love. We can no longer escape it.
> We can no longer escape from one another.
>
> Love is no longer a theme for eloquence, or a way of
>   life for a few to choose whose hearts can decide it.
> It is the sternest necessity; the unequivocal ultimatum.
> There is no other way out; there is no country we can flee to.
> There is no man on earth who must not face this task now.[3]

We are so made that if we do not love we perish. What the law of gravity is to the sun and the stars love is to every human being. It is the profoundest practical need of mankind. It is the life principle of society. In a world relying more and more on force it seems the weakest of instruments, but in reality it is the strongest, for—as in the fable of the sun and the wind—it gains victories force can never gain. There is a more poignant fable which tells how in all the world there was only one thing that could melt adamant, only one liquid potent enough to dissolve the everlasting rock—blood from a human heart. Human souls are more susceptible to love than to any other influence. Love alone can overcome hate. "Love can outlast anything. It is, in fact, the one thing that still stands when all else has fallen."

How can we learn to love? Two sentences from the New Testament provide the answer. "The Son of God who loved me gave himself for me." "We love because he first loved us."

NOTES

[1] From a lecture delivered at Columbia University. *New York Times,* November 16, 1950, p. 29.

[2] Reported in the *New York Times,* December 27, 1954.

[3] Peggy Pond Church, "Ultimatum," in *Fellowship,* April, 1949, a publication of the Fellowship of Reconciliation, Nyack, N.Y. Used with permission.